HOTSPOTS
IONIA

Lefkas, Kefalonia, Zante & Paxos
Also includes Parga & Athens

Written by Christopher Catling, updated by John Earwaker
Front cover photography courtesy of Thomas Cook Tour Operations Ltd

Original design concept by Studio 183 Limited
Series design by the Bridgewater Book Company
Cover design/artwork by Lee Biggadike, Studio 183 Limited

Produced by the Bridgewater Book Company
The Old Candlemakers, West Street, Lewes, East Sussex BN7 2NZ, United Kingdom
www.bridgewaterbooks.co.uk
Project Editor: Emily Casey Bailey
Project Designer: Lisa McCormick

Published by Thomas Cook Publishing
A division of Thomas Cook Tour Operations Limited
PO Box 227, Units 15-16, Coningsby Road, Peterborough PE3 8SB, United Kingdom
email: books@thomascook.com
www.thomascookpublishing.com
+ 44 (0) 1733 416477

ISBN-13: 978-1-84157-541-4
ISBN-10: 1-84157-541-0

First edition © 2006 Thomas Cook Publishing
Text © 2006 Thomas Cook Publishing
Maps © 2006 Thomas Cook Publishing
Project Editor: Diane Ashmore
Production/DTP Editor: Steven Collins

Printed and bound in Spain by Graficas Cems, Navarra, Spain

All rights reserved. No part of this publication may be reproduced, stored in a retrieval
system or transmitted, in any form or by any means, electronic, mechanical, recording
or otherwise, in any part of the world, without prior permission of the publisher.
Requests for permission should be made to the publisher at the above address.

Although every care has been taken in compiling this publication, and the contents
are believed to be correct at the time of printing, Thomas Cook Tour Operations
Limited cannot accept any responsibility for errors or omission, however caused,
or for changes in details given in the guidebook, or for the consequences of any
reliance on the information provided. Descriptions and assessments are based on
the author's views and experiences when writing and do not necessarily represent
those of Thomas Cook Tour Operations Limited.

CONTENTS

SYMBOLS KEY

The following is a key to the symbols used throughout this book:

ℹ	information office	🛡	police station	🍴	restaurant
🚌	bus stop	✈	airport	☕	café
✚	hospital	🏪	supermarket	🍸	bar
✉	post office	↘	tip	◉	fine dining
✝	church	🛍	shopping		

t telephone	**f** fax	**e** email	**W** website address
a address	**L** opening times	**I** important	
€ budget price	€€ mid-range price	€€€ most expensive	
★ special interest	★★ see if passing	★★★ special interest	

INTRODUCTION
Getting to know Ionian Greece

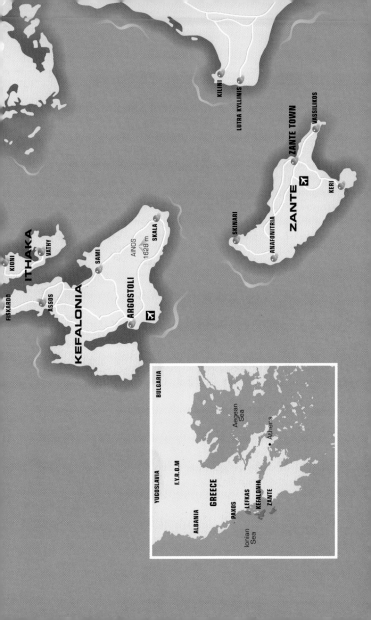

Getting to know Ionian Greece

The Ionian Islands have been celebrated since the time of Homer for their beautiful beaches, pine-clad mountains and dramatic coastline. Rising out of the blue Ionian Sea, midway between Greece and Italy, these fertile islands are clothed in a tapestry of vineyards, olive groves, orchards and wheat fields, creating a patchwork of colour that sets them apart from the barren rocky terrain of many of their Grecian neighbours. Rain falls reliably from November to March, and is the reason for the islands' lush semi-tropical vegetation, but nobody need fear that rain will ruin their holiday: the Ionian Islands are blessed by sunny skies, warm seas and balmy evenings during the holiday season.

There are seven main islands in the Ionian group. Kefalonia, an island still relatively new to tourism, is the biggest, followed by Corfu (not covered in this guide). Lefkas and Zante are popular for their pretty villages and sandy beaches. Ithaka is the legendary home of Odysseus, hero of Homer's Odyssey; together with tiny Paxos and Kythira, it makes an excellent day-trip destination from the bigger islands.

SEA & MOUNTAINS

All the Ionian Islands are rugged and mountainous. Most of the fishing ports and farming villages cling to the sheltered eastern coast, where most of the holiday resorts are also found. Travelling westward, the terrain becomes steeper and wilder, sometimes ending in spectacular cliffs which plummet up to 200 m (approximately 650 ft) into the waves below. Despite this, some of the finest beaches are on the west coast, and it is well worth taking a trip by boat or overland to seek out some private sandy cove hidden amongst the rocks of the craggy coastline.

The islands are also ideal for water sports. North-westerly winds, rising in the afternoon, provide excellent conditions for sailing and windsurfing. If you have never tried either sport, this is the place to do it.

● *The lush Ionian countryside*

CASTLES & POETS

At various times the Ionian Islands were ruled by Venice and by Britain, and both rulers have left their distinctive mark on the region. The Venetians conquered the islands in the 14th century and built castles and harbours to protect their shipping. The practical British built most of the islands' roads.

During the period known to the Greeks as the 'Dark Ages' painters came to the Ionian Islands for the freedom to practise their art, escaping from repressive Turkish rule in other parts of Greece. Churches on the islands are filled with their glowing frescos, painted in the distinctive style of the Ionian School. Poets came here too, and Zante Town proudly celebrates the achievements of Dionysios Solomos, who wrote the words of the Greek national anthem, the Hymn to Freedom.

TURTLES

Sandy beaches can become nesting sites for loggerhead turtles during the June to September breeding season, particularly on Zante (see page 58) and Kefalonia (see page 38). Efforts are now being made to protect these magnificent creatures, which grow to 1 m (3 ft) in length.

WALKING & WILDLIFE

Many of the roads built by the British survive as cobbled tracks, which are used by walkers and cyclists. This is the ideal way to explore the lush Ionian countryside. Nature is at its most abundant in summer, when yellow broom, purple bougainvillaea and red/pink oleanders abound. Wild orchids are relatively common, as are prickly pear cacti. Dancing among the flowers you will find swallowtails and painted lady butterflies. Rocks and walls abound with green and brown lizards, and geckos are a common sight indoors, where they cling to walls looking for flies. Another harmless climber is the tree frog, which turns green or brown to match its habitat.

The best of Ionian Greece

LEFKAS

The least developed of the Ionian Islands with traditional villages and harbourside resorts, Lefkas is named after the ancient Greek word leukos, meaning 'white', on account of the snowy white limestone mountains. Away from the developed area around the capital, the island offers stunning landscapes, unspoiled beaches and relaxed hiking. While on Lefkas:

- learn to windsurf in Vassiliki Bay on the island's south coast, for many the best windsurfing beach in Europe (see page 24);
- swim in the clear blue waters of Porto Katsiki, a brilliant white-sand beach framed by white limestone cliffs (see page 31);
- take a boat trip and dream of owning one of the many offshore islands, such as Skorpios, home of the Onassis family (see page 22).

PARGA

This charming coastal town in northern Greece consists of a crescent of red-tiled houses tumbling down a series of terraces to a sea dotted with rocky outcrops and islets. Parga's lovely beaches are enticing, but it is also ideal for exploring historic mainland Greece. You can:

- wander around the ruins of Nikopolis, the city built by Octavian to celebrate his defeat of Antony and Cleopatra (see page 37)
- take a boat along the River Styx (River Acheron) on the route that ancient pilgrims took to consult with the dead (see page 33)
- explore Ioannina, the ancient capital of Epirus, once ruled by the ambitious Ali Pasha, and buy silverwork in the bazaar (see page 36)
- see the rock formations at Perama, the biggest cave system in Greece (see page 36)
- visit the impressive remains of the ancient oracle and theatre at Dodoni, featuring ancient Greek theatre productions (see page 36).

KEFALONIA

Kefalonia is the largest of the Ionian Islands but the resorts are comparatively small and unobtrusive, enabling visitors to slip into the relaxed rhythms of local life. Highlights include:

- sunbathing at Myrtos, the best beach in the entire Ionian Islands (see page 57)
- taking a daytrip to Fiskardo, stopping for lunch in a taverna overlooking the harbour (see page 56)
- exploring the spectacular Drogarati Cave and boating on the underground Melissani Lake, island hopping to Ithaka, Zante, Lefkas and the mainland (see page 56).

ZANTE

The southernmost island of the Ionian group, Zante offers glorious beaches, plenty of nightlife and stunning seascapes. In Zante be sure to:

- sunbathe at Laganas (see page 67), Vassilikos (see page 72), Alykes (see page 76) and Tsilivi (see page 79)
- shop for rugs, bedspreads and tablecloths at Volimes (see page 82)

- visit Anafonitrias monastery where the island's patron saint, Dionysios, lived out his last days as abbot (see page 82)
- watch spectacular sunsets at Kampi and swim at Smuggler's Cove against a backdrop of dazzling white cliffs (see page 82).

PAXOS

Tiny Paxos retains a traditional character in spite of its proximity to Corfu and visitors easily adopt the islanders' laid-back lifestyle when visiting pretty villages or relaxing in waterside tavernas. Highlights include:

- Gaios, the Venetian-style capital, for nightlife (see page 86)
- Voutoumi beach at Anti-Paxos for swimming in turquoise lagoons (see page 91)
- Lakka (see page 88) and Loggos (see page 90), picturesque harbours by deserted beaches and peaceful olive groves
- the stunning caves on the west coast (see page 91).

MAINLAND GREECE

Day trips from Lefkas, Parga and Zante allow you to to explore both Olympia and Athens. Olympia is the birthplace of the Olympic Games, and where the Olympic torch is still lit (see page 92). Athens, the capital of Greece, is famous for its ancient ruins (see page 92). Shopping in the old Plaka district and watching the Changing of the Evzone Guards complete the Greek experience (see page 94).

SPELLING

There is no commonly applied system for spelling Greek place names, so you will find a variety of different versions on maps and signs. We have used the accepted English spellings in this book, but you may also come across the following:

- Lefkada for Lefkas
- Cephallonia, Kefallinia or Kefallonia for Kefalonia
- Zakinthos or Zakynthos for Zante

RESORTS
The islands & excursions

THE ISLAND OF LEFKAS

N

IONIAN SEA

0   5 km
0   1   2   3 miles

TSOUKALADES

LEFKAS TOWN

SANTA MAURA

GREECE

• Aghios Nikitas

KARIOTES

Kathisma

LYGIA

• Kalamitsi   • Karia

NIKIANA

• Englouvi

PERIGALI

MT ELATI
1158 m

NIDRI

SPARTI
MADOURI
SKORPIDI
SKORPIOS

LEFKAS

ATHANI

AGHIOS
PETROS   SIVROS

VLYHO
DESSIMI

VATHY

SPARTOCHORI   KATOMERI

Egremeni

POROS

301m

Pórto
Katsiki

VASSILIKI   Sivota •

MEGANISSI

Agiofili

Papanikolis
Sea Cave

Cape Lefkatas

Lefkas Town
capital of Lefkas

Lefkas Town (also known as Lefkada) sits at the northernmost tip of Lefkas island, separated from mainland Greece by a lagoon known as the Ichthiotrofrio – literally, 'the fish pond' – where herons and pelicans wade in search of food. Though flattened by an earthquake in 1953, the town has a great deal of charm because of its narrow traffic-free alleys. As a precaution against further earthquakes, many houses were built with timber upper storeys, with pretty wooden balconies and tiny gardens.

The main street, **Odhos Dörpfeld** (also known as Idanou Mela), is named after the late 19th-century archaeologist who spent much of his private income on excavations in the fruitless attempt to find the palace of Odysseus, hero of Homer's *Odyssey*. In and around this street you will find most of the town's popular bars and restaurants, which bustle with life in the summer, when many mainland Greek holidaymakers drive over to the island.

 The sun can be very fierce by midday, but there are plenty of shady cafés in Lefkas' Main Square, where you can relax and watch the world go by over delicious cakes and cool drinks.

IS LEFKAS AN ISLAND?
Lefkas was attached to mainland Greece by a narrow strip of land until the 6th century BC, when a canal was dug through the isthmus, turning what had been part of the mainland into an island. Today Lefkas is connected to the mainland by a bridge, which opens every hour, on the hour, to let boats through. You can walk across the causeway to explore the ruins of Santa Maura castle on the mainland, originally built in the 14th century.

SHOPPING

The best place for souvenir shopping is the pedestrian precinct in **Odhos Dörpfeld**, off the Main Square. You will find plenty of small shops selling ceramics, pottery, and local food.

THINGS TO SEE & DO

Archaeological Museum ★★

The best of the objects found by Dörpfeld during his excavations on Lefkas are now in the National Museum in Athens, so this one-room museum consists of the leftovers: pottery, lamps, statues, axes and architectural sculpture dating from as far back as the 12th century BC.
ⓐ Aggelou Sikelianou & N. Svoronou Streets ❶ 26450 23678
🕓 Open Tues–Sun 09.00–13.00 ❶ Admission €2

Churches ★★

Lefkas has several fine frescos painted by members of the Ionian School of artists, who were influenced by Italian Renaissance painting, and whose work is often more naturalistic than that of their contemporaries. Their work is to be found in private chapels, with erratic opening hours (try and get in just after the daily service). The best examples are in the churches of **Aghios Dhimitrios** (ⓐ Zabelion Street), the churches of the **Pantokrator** and **Theotokou** (ⓐ Both on Dörpfeld) and **Aghios Minas** (ⓐ On the junction of Ioannou Mela and Merarchias).

Faneromeni Monastery ★★

This pretty timber-built monastery, with a museum and small chapel full of colourful stained glass, was originally built in the 17th century. Hanging in the courtyard is a log that was beaten to call the monks to prayer during the war, when the ringing of bells was banned by the German occupiers, fearful that the monks would use the bells to transmit coded messages. ⓐ 4 km (2¹/₂ miles) outside Lefkas
🕓 Open 08.00–14.00 and 16.00–20.00 ❶ Admission free

Folklore Museum ★★

Island life is illustrated through a small collection of festive embroidered costumes, furniture and domestic items. Also on display are photographs of the town before the destructive 1953 earthquake, and models of some of the prehistoric settlements uncovered by the archaeologist Dörpfeld in the 19th century. ⓐ 2 Stefanitsi, Filarmonikis ❶ 26450 22473 ⓛ Open daily 10.00–13.00 and 18.00–21.00 (summer) ❶ Admission charge

Phonograph Museum ★★

Small museum just behind Café Baloo, south of Lefkas' Main Square, containing a zany selection of early gramophones, plus cameras, photographs and jewellery boxes dating from between 1850 and 1920. Also displayed are old portraits and bank notes. The museum sells cassettes of old-time music too. ⓐ Kalkanou Street ⓛ Open 09.00–13.00 and 18.00–23.00 ❶ Admission free

BEACHES

Just west of the town, the 4 km- (2¹/₂ mile) long sand and shingle beach of **Vira** (**Gyra**) is big enough to accommodate all visitors. Beyond the windmill is a second beach, named **Aghios Ioannis Antzousis** after the nearby Crusader chapel. Further south are the two sandy beaches of **Kathisma** and **Pefkoulia**.

RESTAURANTS & BARS (see map on page 16)

Café Agora € ❶ Popular coffee and sweet shop which also serves ouzo, ice creams, toast and sandwiches. Trendy atmosphere and popular with locals and great views of everyday Greek life. ⓐ 101 Odhos Dörpfeld ❶ 26450 23580

Café Karfakis € ❷ Lovely old-fashioned bar decorated with old photographs, which maintains the tradition of serving little morsels of food – mezedes – with your drinks. ⓐ 125 Odhos Dörpfeld ❶ 26450 26730

Café Zygos €€ ❸ Fashionable location overlooking the water. Trendy clientele. Relaxed atmosphere. Try the delicious range of cocktails. ⓐ Aggelou Sikelianou

Gustoso €€ ❹ Popular with Greeks and holidaying Italians, this restaurant specialises in pasta, pizzas and a range of ice creams and cocktails. Also provides a take-away service. ⓐ Aggelou Sikelianou ❶ 26450 24603

Kato Vrysi €€ ❺ Traditional taverna serving homely dishes, including moussaka and various Greek-style salads. ⓐ Dörpfeld

Lighthouse €€ ❻ Delightful garden and a good choice of local dishes. ⓐ 14 Filarmonikis ❶ 26450 25117

Romantika €€ ❼ Huge menu covering everything from seafood, steaks and salads to typical Greek taverna food. Nightly performances of local folk song in the high season. ⓐ 11 Mitropoleos ❶ 26450 22235

Voglia di Pizza €€€ ❽ Up-market restaurant on the waterfront serving Greek and Italian dishes in cool and sophisticated ambience. ⓐ Aggelou Sikelianou ❶ 26450 26461

NIGHTLIFE

The liveliest nightspots are in and around the harbour end of Dörpfeld, where you will be spoiled for choice by the number of bars and cafés competing for your custom, most with pavement tables spilling out on to the street. The best place for open-air music and dancing is **Club Milos** on Yira beach. The most enjoyable spot to spend a summer evening is **Platia Aghios Spiridon** where, during the two-week Folklore Festival in August, buskers entertain the crowds who gather here to drink and eat in the bars and restaurants that line three sides of the square.

Lygia
a tranquil fishing port

Lygia (pronounced 'Lig-yah'), just 5 km (3 miles) south of Lefkas Town, has an attractive harbour and looks across to the ancient fortress of Aghios Georgios (St George) on the mainland. The pace of life is slow and relaxed with just a couple of hotels, supermarkets and restaurants, which are strung unpretentiously along the 2 km (1¼ mile) stretch of resort.

To the south of the fishing port is a small shingly beach backed by shady trees and within walking distance of some very attractive waterside fish tavernas, where you can watch fishermen bring in their catch. Further north is the hamlet of Kariotes, noted for the weekly Wednesday clothing market beside the village square. For nightlife it is better to head to the clubs and bars in Lefkas Town, or to neighbouring Nidri if you want to book any boat trips.

 A pre-breakfast stroll to the small fishing port, as the sun rises on the boats coming back from the sea, is a fine way to start the day, and a good place to take photographs for idyllic holiday memories.

THINGS TO SEE & DO
Island hopping ★★★
Board the **Nicolaous** cruise boat at Nidri for a fabulous day out along the coast of Lefkas and neighbouring islands. Visit Meganissi with the sea cave of Papanikolis and picturesque Spartochori, and cruise to Skorpios island, owned by the Onassis family and the former home of Jackie Kennedy Onassis.

Forgotten Islands ★★★
Spend a day on the sailing boat **Christina**, discovering the islands of Kastos and Kalamos. Relax in Kastos village harbour with its 17th-century Agia Ioannis church. At lunchtime, the boat anchors in a secluded bay for

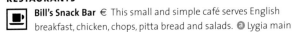

swimming and an onboard buffet lunch. The day rounds off with time in Kalamos village, before smooth sailing back into Nidri.

BEACHES

Further south there are some fine beaches and wonderful views of the mainland at **Nikiana** and at **Perigali**.

RESTAURANTS

Bill's Snack Bar € This small and simple café serves English breakfast, chicken, chops, pitta bread and salads. ⓐ Lygia main road ☎ 26450 71556

Green Stop €€ Welcoming restaurant with waterside views. Specialises in pizzas, pasta and traditional Greek meals. ⓐ Lygia main road

To Limani €€ Fish taverna right next door to O Xouras with waterside location. Friendly service and good value. ⓐ Lygia port

Old Navy € This fast-food outlet does great take-away kebabs, chicken and chips and steaks. ⓐ Lygia main road

Sidrivani Taverna € Look no further for typical Greek food. Everything from traditional grills, fried kalamari and authentic horiatiki (Greek salad with enormous chunks of feta cheese) and rough brown bread in this taverna overlooking a shaded square. ⓐ Kariotes

O Xouras €€ This fish taverna, which means 'the barber', offers a good range of freshly caught fish. You can eat in or out on tables right beside the waterfront. ⓐ Lygia port ☎ 26450 71312 ⓛ Open for lunch and dinner until 03.00

Yianni's Taverna €€ Good-value grilled meats and mezedes. Overlooking the sea. ⓐ Lygia main road ☎ 26450 71407

◉ *Nidri's shingle beaches have a laid-back feel*

Nidri
relaxed and easy

Nidri lies to the south of Lefkas, the island capital, on the east coast and enjoys lovely views of the wooded islets of Sparti, Madouri, Skorpidi and Skorpios. Although Nidri is Lefkas' busiest and biggest resort town, with a good choice of shops, it is still pretty laid back compared with other popular islands yet retains the feel of traditional Greece. The nightlife is lively with waterfront bars and restaurants and a couple of late-night discos.

THINGS TO SEE & DO
Boat trips ★ ★ ★

Head for the quay in Nidri and choose from any number of boats to take you on a tour of the delightful offshore islands. Most of the boats are motorised launches with bars and toilets. Alternatively, you can take the public ferry from Nidri to Meganissi.

The closest island is privately owned Madouri, followed by uninhabited Sparti. The island of Skorpios, where Aristotle Onassis the Greek shipping magnate married Jackie Kennedy and where he is buried, is now owned by his granddaughter. Some boats encircle Skorpios while others drop anchor to let you swim. Some trips call in at the small port of Spilio on Meganissi, where the main attraction is the sea cave at Papanikolis.

Rachi Waterfall ★★★

Pack your towel and costume and try the 90-minute stroll from Nidri to the hamlet of Rachi for a cooling dip in a natural pool below these pretty waterfalls. The way to Rachi is signposted from the centre of Nidri. Take plenty of water to drink as there is only one taverna on the way.

BEACHES

Nidri's two beaches are narrow and shingly and can get crowded during July and August. Smaller beaches can be found around the bay but for a less crowded alternative, head to **Dessimi**, a sandy beach to the south of Nidri.

RESTAURANTS

 Athos Chinese Restaurant €€€ Nidri's only Chinese restaurant set by the pool of the Athos Hotel. ❷ Nidri main road ❶ 26450 92384 ⏱ Open for dinner only

 Catamaran €€ Fashionable hangout and ultra-cool ambience. Greek and Italian food. ❷ Nidri waterfront ❶ 26450 92146

 La Dolce Vita €€ First-class Italian food cooked by Italian chef. ❷ Nidri waterfront ⏱ Open 18.00–late

 Gelateria di Paris € Relaxing open-air gelateria serving pizzas, crepes, waffles, ices, cakes, coffees and cocktails, with music. ❷ Nidri waterfront ❶ 26450 92235

 George's Place €€ Greek taverna run by lively local called George. Try the gyros (sliced pork kebabs with salad, chips and tzatiki rolled in pitta bread). Sometimes George does handstands on the table! ❷ Nidri main road ❶ 26450 92689

Il Sappore €€ Pizzas and pastas in every imaginable form. ❷ Nidri waterfront ❶ 26450 92915

Vassiliki
a windsurfer's paradise

Vassiliki is 16 km (10 miles) south west of Nidri and lies in a huge bay sheltered by mountains. Although the pebble beach may not be ideal for swimming, for windsurfing it is regarded as one of the best in Europe. The bay is alive with brightly coloured sails skimming across the water and there are plenty of places offering tuition and equipment if you come unprepared.

🔺 *Vassiliki is great for windsurfing and boat trips*

The breezes, which make Vassiliki so perfect for windsurfing, are just right for beginners in the morning, grow stronger as the day goes on, and then die down by dusk. The narrow streets of the tiny village bustle with visitors and the lively nightlife draws young people from all over the island.

THINGS TO SEE & DO
Boat trips ★ ★ ★
Water-taxis leave from Vassiliki harbour to the white cliffs of Cape Lefkatas (see page 30) and the pretty white beach of Agiofili. The waters at Agiofili are crystal clear and perfect for snorkelling. Take your own food and drink as there are no facilities, although sunbeds and parasols are available for hire. An inter-island ferry to Kefalonia also leaves throughout the day.

Land activities ★
Try horse riding or rent bicycles, mountain bikes and cars to explore the olive groves and flower fields around **Syvros**, one of the bigger villages to the north. Ask your tour rep, hotel or the tourist office for details.

BEACHES
There is a pebble beach near the Apollos Hotel. The best beach is at **Ponti** at the northern side of Vassiliki bay, where a water sports centre offers windsurfing and water-skiing.

SHOPPING
Vassiliki is a popular backwater for local artists. For postcards, pottery, jewellery, ceramics and unique examples of local art, head for the shop called **Katoi** (❸ On the Ponti Road, next door to Mythos Taverna ❶ 26450 31700).

RESTAURANTS

 Alexanders €€ Take your pick from Greek traditional cuisine and take in the harbour views at the same time.

 Dina's € Huge selection of organic pastries, ice cream and rice puddings. Try the tiropitta (cheese pie) with a Greek salad for a lunchtime snack. ❷ Vassiliki waterfront ❶ 26450 31396

 Dolphin Restaurant € Traditional cuisine such as fish soup, swordfish and grills served on outside tables decked in green and white table-cloths. ❷ Vassiliki waterfront ❶ 26450 31430

 Elena € Popular streetside coffee shop serving English breakfast. Good choice of ice cream, cakes, croissants and tiropitta. ❷ Vassiliki waterfront ❶ 26450 31890

 Evi's Pirate Palace €€ Popular venue for wide range of English and Greek meals, drinks and snacks. Also noted for special cocktails and good views of the street from flower-clad courtyard. ❸ Port road

To Kima € Wonderful views across the bay from this beachside taverna serving food and drink all day. ❸ Ponti ❶ 26450 31303

Mythos Taverna € Friendly taverna serving excellent cocktails and good international and Greek fare. Try the local wine or choose from The Godfather, The Godmother or the Sicilian Kiss cocktails. ❸ Across the road from Vassiliki Camping ❶ 26450 31414

Restaurant Sapfo €€ Lively atmosphere especially during the evening when you can feast on great grills, pastas or mezedes.

Stelios Taverna € Baked vegetables, lamb and peppered steaks are just some examples of the extensive menu in this waterfront taverna. ❷ Vassiliki waterfront ❶ 26450 31581

Vangelaras € Excellent grills with harbour views. Open for English breakfast right through to dinner or when the last customer leaves. ⓐ Vassiliki waterfront ❶ 26450 31224

The best view of Vassiliki port while sipping a drink is from the smart Ponti Beach Hotel above the bay. Spiros supermarket nearby sells basics like bread, pies, fruit, beach goods and souvenirs.

🔺 *Vassiliki is ideal for sailing*

Lefkas excursions
mountains and coves

Lygia and Nidri both make an excellent base for exploring the island. Inland, you can visit ancient churches with time-worn frescos and mountain villages, where the womenfolk create delicate lace and embroidery following centuries-old traditions. The sandy beaches of the west and south coasts, tucked into coves between the wild limestone cliffs of the western shores, are ideal for every kind of water sports activity. For a longer excursion, take the bus to Athens (see page 92), where the bustle of the modern Greek capital contrasts poignantly with the majestic remains of the ancient Greek acropolis.

LACE VILLAGES
Karia ★★

Karia is the main production centre for the lace and embroidery that is sold all over the island, and there is an excellent selection here of hand-made products, as well as carpets and other textiles. Even if you do not want to shop, the mountain village is worth visiting for its excellent folklore museum, the **Museum Maria Koutsochero** (🕒 Open daily 09.00–18.00 ❶ Admission charge), run by a long-established family of lacemakers. Housed in a typical peasant's home, the furnishings, equipment and utensils give you a good idea of a village way of life that only just survives.

The tree-shaded main square has a number of bars and restaurants, and a tea shop where you can have English tea and toasted sandwiches. In August, a re-enactment of a Greek wedding party takes place in the square; a bride and groom parade through the village on horseback, wine flows, and there is plenty of merriment. Karia is 8 km (5 miles) south of Lefkas.

▶ *Pórto Katsiki's glorious beach*

BOWLING WITH EGGS

The game of *t'ambáli* is very popular on Lefkas. Similar to the French game of *boules*, this version, unique to the island, is fiendishly difficult because it is played with egg-shaped balls. To make matters more complicated, the game is not played on level ground, but on a saucer-shaped, concave surface.

Englouvi ★★

Close to Karia is Englouvi, another lace village and the highest settlement on Lefkas (730 m/2400 ft above sea level). Set in a green valley on the slopes of Mount Elati (1158 m/3800 ft), the village is famous for its green lentils, prized all over Greece, and during August free lentils and home-baked bread are offered to visitors.

THE WESTERN & SOUTHERN COASTS
Aghios Nikitas ★★★

With its jumble of timber-clad buildings spilling down the bottom of a gorge to a pebble beach, Aghios Nikitas is easily the most photogenic and picturesque village on Lefkas. Flowers and vines hang from balconies along the narrow street, and provide shade for the terraces of old tavernas. You can swim here in the refreshingly cool and crystal-clear waters below the village or take a sea-taxi to the long sandy beach at nearby Mylos.

Kalamitsi ★★

Kalamitsi is reached along steep roads with many a hairpin bend. The views from this typical mountain village are best appreciated over a drink or lunch in one of the traditional tavernas and the shops are well stocked with souvenirs, such as locally made embroidery.

Cape Lefkatas ★★★

Also known as Cape Doukato, the gleaming white rock at the southwesternmost tip of the island is the original Lovers' Leap. It was from here that Sappho, the ancient Greek poetess, threw herself into the waves. Although she was better known as a lesbian (the term derives from Lesbos, the island of Sappho's birth), it was her unrequited love for a man – the handsome Phaeon – that drove her to her suicide. Today a lighthouse tops the 60 m (197 ft) high rock, from which people still hurl themselves, though nowadays they are usually strapped to a hang-glider.

Sivota ★★

Sivota, a quiet fishing village on the south coast between Vassiliki and Nidri with a string of fish tavernas, is a safe anchorage for yachtsmen. You can have pleasant strolls around the bay watching fishermen unload their catch and spreading out their nets to dry. But for the best views, make your way to the top of the cliff where a taverna perched on the cliffside overlooks the bay.

BEACHES
Egremeni

Reached by 260 steep steps from the road that runs across the top of Cape Lefkatas, Egremeni has a fine sandy beach, though it, too, becomes crowded by mid-morning as visitors arrive by boat from Vassiliki. Egremeni is at the south-western tip of the island.

Kathisma

Kathisma is a sandy beach that lies south of Aghios Nikitas. From here a winding road continues southwards to Cape Lefkatas remarkable for its coastal and mountain scenery. The road dips into valleys, climbs into the mountains and swings down into bays with sandy beaches.

Porto Katsiki

A rock slide in 1998 caused the beach to be cut in two, but the clear blue waters and white shingle beach, framed by white cliffs, still make Porto Katsiki one of the best beaches on Lefkas. Most people arrive by boat from Vassiliki, but you can get there by descending 60 steps from the main road. Mobile food stalls sell drinks and snacks, which tend to be expensive, so it is better to take your own with you.

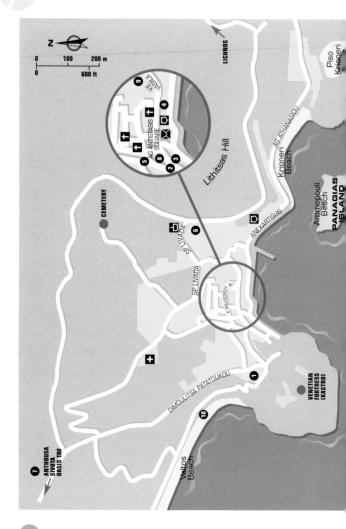

Parga
mountains & olive groves

Parga (rhymes with lager) is a charming and atmospheric resort set in a large bay on the Greek mainland, backed by mountains clad in olive groves and stands of green pine. As the main resort for the Epirus region of north-western Greece, Parga is a busy holiday town, with plenty of life, but one where the traditional Greek way of life has not been spoiled by tourism.

Parga's bustling harbour is lined with restaurants, bars and nightspots, while behind is a labyrinth of narrow cobbled alleys lined with traditional red-tiled houses, stretching up to the Venetian fortress. This massive fortress, known as the Kastro, was built in 1642 on the site of a building destroyed in 1537. The fortress commands fine views over the harbour and out to the rocky islets scattered across the bay.

Parga's attractions include cruises southwards along the coast to the mouth of the **River Acheron**, which the ancient Greeks believed was the **River Styx** – the river that souls had to cross before entering Hades – where legend has it that swimming makes you look 20 years younger, and a visit to the turquoise waters of Aphrodite's Caves.

BEACHES
Krioneri and Piso Krioneri
These two small beaches lie within walking distance of Parga Town. Umbrellas and sunbeds are for hire.

Lichnos
Clean, quiet and lying in a deep tree-clad bay, Lichnos attracts day-trippers who arrive in water-taxis from Parga Town. You can water-ski from the water sports centre right on the beach and learn all the techniques of wakeboarding (being towed behind a powerful boat and using its wake to pull off a range of stunts and tricks). Tavernas and restaurants provide snacks and meals 3 km (2 miles) south east of Parga Town.

Valtos

Parga's best beach, Valtos, consists of a 1.5 km-long (1 mile) stretch of pebble and sand just beyond the Venetian fortress to the south west. The beach is easily reached by a 20-minute stroll through olive groves from the town centre, or you can take a water-taxi from Parga Harbour (every 30 minutes from 09.00). Facilities include windsurfing and parascending.

RESTAURANTS & BARS (see map on page 32)

Andreas €€ ❶ Welcoming taverna serving Italian and Greek fare situated in quiet location near the castle. ❸ Near the ramparts of the castle ❶ 26840 32057

Blue Bar €€ ❷ Cocktails, fancy ice creams and drinks in lively atmosphere near the castle. Cool and sophisticated. Arguably the best views of the harbour. ❸ On the way to the castle at the top of the steps at Gaki Zeri Street ❶ 26840 32067

Eden Crêperie Café Bar € ❸ Excellent waffles and crêpes in informal atmosphere. Buzzing at night. ❸ 26 Dimitriou, Parga ❶ 26840 31409

● *Parga's bay is scattered with rocky outcrops*

Flamingo € ❹ Delicious delicatessen and pastries, coffees and huge range of cocktails in this popular bar. ❸ Next door to Parga police station ❶ 26840 32207

Istros €€ ❺ Choose from a range of coffees with creamy chocolate or almond cake or Greek desserts in this cafeteria. ❸ Mayromihali Street, Parga ❶ 26840 31798

Kineziko €€ ❻ Parga's only Chinese restaurant perched on a hill behind the town. Excellent service and food and good value for money. ❸ On the eastern edge of town at the end of Spirou Livada Street ❶ 26840 32458

Oasis € ❼ Lovely garden setting away from the bustle of Parga. Take your pick from what's on offer from delicious tiropittakia, fried courgettes and aubergines. Large parking area beneath olive trees. ❸ Village centre, Anthousa, 3 km (1.8 miles) from Parga ❶ 26840 31396

Restaurant Castello €€€ ❽ Highly regarded and up-market courtyard restaurant, forming part of the Acropol Hotel, located 150 m (165 yds) from the harbour. ❸ Aghios Apostolon 4 ❶ 26840 31239

Taka Taka Mam € ❾ Original Greek taverna and cuisine in street setting. Take your pick from the kitchen. Very good stifado and wine from the barrel. ❸ 11 Alexandrou Baka, Parga ❶ 26840 32286

Yacht Club €€ ❿ Convivial snack bar and restaurant beside Valtos Beach. Serves pizzas, salads, omelettes, club sandwiches and hamburgers on outdoor tables shaded with umbrellas. ❸ Valtos Beach, Parga ❶ 26840 32241

 Parga's best disco is **Camares**, on VE Vasila Street, one block back from the waterfront. ❶ 26840 32000

EXCURSIONS
Corfu and Paxos ★★★
Excursion boats for Corfu leave from Parga, allowing you to visit the Archaeological Museum, the New and Old Fortress, the splendid St Spiridon Church and to shop in Corfu Town. For uncomplicated Greek life, take in the small islands of Paxos (see page 91) and Anti-Paxos (see page 99), or cruise around them, calling at bays and coves for a swim in the crystal waters.

Ioannina, Dodoni and Perama Caves ★★★
Day trips from Parga can be made to visit Ioannina, the ancient capital of the Epirus region 150 km (90 miles) north east of Parga. Ioannina has a bustling bazaar and is the place to shop for modern examples of silversmiths' art. Alternatively, you can visit several interesting museums. The small **Museum of Popular Art** (Frourion, the Citadel) has silverwork and tapestries dating back to the reign of Turkish tyrant, Ali Pasha, from 1744–1822 (❶ 26510 78062 ❷ Open Mon–Fri 08.00–21.00 and Sat–Sun 09.00–20.00 in summer; Mon–Fri 08.00–15.00 and Sat–Sun 09.00–15.00 in winter ❶ Admission charge). The **Byzantine Museum** (Frourion, the Citadel), has a reconstruction of a silversmith's workshop (❶ 26510 25989 ❷ Open Tues–Sun 08.00–19.00 in summer; Tues–Sun 08.30–17.00 in winter ❶ Admission charge).

Water-taxis make the journey across Lake Ioannina to the small island of **Nissaki**, noted for its 13th-century monastery and the room where Ali Pasha was executed. About 5 km (3 miles) north of Ioannina at **Perama** is the biggest cave system in Greece, where guided tours lead you past illuminated stalactite and stalagmite formations (❶ 26510 81521 ❷ Open 08.00–20.00 in summer; until 16.00 in winter ❶ Admission charge)

The **Oracle of Dodoni**, 22 km (14 miles) south west of Ioannina, dating back to the 3rd century bc, became famous because the ancient Greeks believed that it contained the voice of the great god Zeus. Today, impressive remains of a Roman town survive, including the theatre, the biggest in Greece and still used for summer performances (❶ 26510 82287 ❷ Open 08.30–19.00 in summer; 08.30–17.00 in winter ❶ Admission charge).

The Nekromanteion of Efyras
(The Gateway to the Underworld) and Kassopi ★★

The **Oracle of Nekromanteion** (built circa 3rd-century BC) is where ancient Greeks communicated with the dead. ❸ 22 km (14 miles) south east of Parga, near the village of Mesopotamos ● Open 08.00–19.00 (summer), 08.00–15.00 (winter) ❶ Admission charge. Further south are the remains of **Kassopi**, a town built in 4th-century BC. In 1803 a group of local women committed suicide here, close to the Zalongo monument, rather than surrender to the approaching Turkish army, just one of many tragic events marking the hostilities that still exist between the peoples of Greece and Turkey ❶ 26810 41026 ● Open Tues–Sun 08.30–15.00 ❶ Admission charge

Preveza ★

A lively waterfront and location of the region's main airport but also noted for the extensive ruins of the city of **Nikopolis**, just 7km (4 miles) to the north. ❸ Preveza is 65 km (40 miles) south of Parga ● The ruins and museum are open Tues–Sun 08.30–15.00 ❶ Admission charge

Zagoria and the Monasteries of Meteora ★★★

If you have time it's worth making the two-day excursion inland to see the traditional villages of Zagoria, passing the wildly photogenic Vikos Gorge (the deepest in Europe) on the way, and overnighting to be up early to watch the sunrise over the monasteries of Meteora. Perched on lofty pillars of precipitous rocks soaring from surrounding plains, these monasteries can be visited to see how monks and nuns live out their vocation, suspended between heaven and earth. The town of Metsovo nearby is a ski resort in winter, but in summer has plenty of tavernas, good for a lunch stop, and opportunities to sample the local cheese, honey, pasta and wine. Meteora is 230 km (140 miles) east of Parga.

For the best views of Parga, follow the road passing Krioneri Beach until you reach a supermarket. Turn right here and follow the steep footpath up to the headland where there is a small church.

THE ISLAND OF KEFALONIA

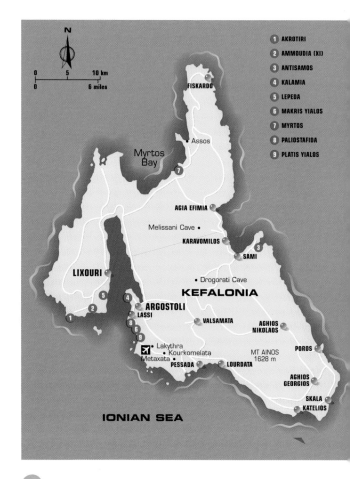

Argostoli
capital of Kefalonia

Tragedy struck Argostoli in 1953 when the graceful island capital was all but destroyed by a major earthquake. Today, all traces of the disaster have disappeared and the town has been rebuilt using some traditional materials. Many attractive older buildings remain, including the gracious mansions along the palm-lined streets to the north of the main square, Platia Vallianou.

Platia Vallianou is the social centre of the town, where local people watch the world go by from pavement café tables. It is also the location of the evening volta, when everyone comes out to stroll, chat with their friends and enjoy the cooler air. Equally good for a stroll is the lively waterfront, with its balconied shops and tavernas. From here there are views across the Koutavos lagoon to the wooded slopes of Mount Evmorfia. Moored in the harbour is a good mix of fishing boats, ferries and tour craft. The tourist office is at the northern end of the seafront promenade, and it is from here that ferries depart every hour for Lixouri (see page 50).

Beyond, the road continues round the peninsula to the resort of Lassi (see page 45). At the southern end of the harbour is the 800 m (2625 ft) Drapanos Bridge, built in 1813 by the Swiss-born British governor of the island, Colonel Philippe de Bosset. Local people initially resisted the causeway's construction, on the grounds that it would bring undesirable elements into the town from the villages on the other side of the lagoon!

THINGS TO SEE & DO
Archaeological Museum ★
Everything you need to know about ancient Kefalonia packed into two rooms, including 3,000-year-old pottery from the Mycenaean period and a statue of Pan, the goat-like god of shepherds and wild things.
ⓐ Georgiou Vergoti ❶ 26710 28300 ◑ Open Tues–Sat 08.30–15.00
❶ Admission charge

DELADETSIMA

VASILLISSIS SOFIAS

Port

N

0   100   200 m
0   600 ft

MOMFERATOU

PAN HAROKOPOU

GERASSIMOU LIVADA

CINE ANNY

NTOG OFFICE

ARGOSTOLI

PLATIA VALLIANOU

Napier Gardens

VALIANOU

FOKAS-COSMETATOS FOUNDATION

LASSI

ARCHAEOLOGICAL MUSEUM

Marina

KORGIALENIO HISTORY & FOLKLORE MUSEUM

ROKOU VERGOTI

ILIA ZERVOU

VIRONOS

XOIDA

MONUMENT

BRITISH CEMETERY

EL VENIZELOU

ILIA ZERVOU

LITHOSTROSOS

IOANNOU METAXA

LASSIS

CATHOLIC CHURCH

GEORGIOU VERGOTI

Road Causeway

DEVOSETOU

Boat excursions ★★★

Take a cruise on a glass-bottomed boat from the harbour to spot dolphins, visit ancient sunken shipwrecks and photograph marine life. Details from Port Authority kiosk on waterfront. ☎ 26710 22224

British Cemetery ★

Dating back to the 1820s and the British Protectorate, though not a War Graves' Commission cemetery, it's worth a visit. ⓐ Fifty metres on right, after crossing Drapano Bridge from Argostoli

Cine Anny Outdoor Cinema ★★

An outdoor garden cinema that's a novel experience if you've never been to an outdoor cinema. It shows current major releases in English, usually in two showings. The late show is best, as during early season, with light evenings, the screen can be indistinct. ⓐ 54 Pan, Argostoli ☎ 26710 25880 ⏰ Open June–Aug only ❶ Admission charge

Fokas Museum (Cosmetatos Foundation) ★★

This museum housing lithographs, coins and a wealth of other historical material is linked with the **Botanica Garden Project** on the edge of town. ⓐ Off Platia Callainou, behind Central Café ⏰ Open Mon–Sat 09.30–13.00 and 19.00–22.00 ❶ Admission charge (ticket includes garden project)

Korgialenio History & Folklore Museum ★★

A well-presented account of island culture and history, shown through a series of reconstructed rooms, from the cave-like poverty of a peasant farmer's dwelling to the richly furnished rooms of a wealthy mansion. ⓐ Ilia Zervou ☎ 26710 22584 ⏰ Open Tues–Sat 09.00–14.00 ❶ Admission charge

BEACHES

The best beaches are at Lassi (see page 45) but you can cool off at the new lido to the north of the town and use the bar and cafeteria (❶ Admission charge).

RESTAURANTS (see map on page 40)

Many good restaurants, bars and tavernas are found around Argostoli's main square and its side streets, or along the harbourfront road called Ioannou Metaxa.

Captains Table €€€ ❶ Upmarket eatery. Try fresh fish or lobster. ⓐ 3 Rizospaton ❶ 26710 23896

Elios € ❷ Friendly family run taverna-café with traditional village-style dishes and mezes. Bouzouki music evenings; popular with both locals and visitors. ⓐ 62a Ioannou Metaxa ❶ 26710 23650

Kalafatis €€ ❸ Old family recipes prepared in a traditional charcoal oven. Enjoy the sea views near the Drapanos Bridge. ⓐ Ioannou Metaxa (seafront) ❶ 26710 22627

Kiani Akti €€€ ❹ Family-run restaurant specialising in mezedes, good wines and ouzo. The restaurant occupies its own jetty to the north of town. Plenty of parking. ⓐ Ioannou Metaxa (seafront) ❶ 26710 26680

Il Platiano €€€ ❺ The Ionion Plaza Hotel's Italian restaurant. Watch the evening volta from the outdoor seating. Extensive menu to suit all appetites, with good local and Italian wine list. ⓐ Platia Vallianou ❶ 26710 25580

Pizza Mella € ❻ Small, modern waterfront pizzeria-café serving an extensive range of pizza toppings and pasta dishes. Fine views across the bay from veranda. ⓐ 36 Ioannou Metaxa, near to sailing club and marina ❶ 26710 24090

Portside €€ ❼ Run by a Greek family that returned from New York in the 1990s, this popular restaurant serves excellent fresh fish and grilled dishes. ⓐ 58 Ioannou Metaxa (seafront) ❶ 26710 24130

Kohenoor Indian Restaurant €€ **8** The only authentic curries on Kefalonia. All your favourites, spiced to your liking on request. Children's menu. 2 Odos Lavragka, off Platia Vallianou 26710 226789

Taverna Diana €€ **9** Excellent moussaka, Kefalonian meat pies and grills in a modern open setting with view of the bay. 54 Ioannou Metaxa, opposite Lixouri ferry port 26710 227788

Taverna Patsouras €€ **10** Popular late-night haunt for hungry Greeks and tourists. Typical Kefalonian fare and fine wines. 32 Ioannou Metaxa (seafront) 26710 22779

Tsilikos € **11** Long-established souvlaki and grill house. Try the chicken or pork gyros. Large portions ideal for hungry eaters. Ioannou Metaxa (seafront) 26710 22304 Open until late

NIGHTLIFE

Bass Club **12** Large, late-night Greek-style clubbing, party theme nights and visiting DJs in high season. Rokou Vergoti 26710 25020

Bodega Cervezeria **13** Modern bar-café with extensive range of popular bottled European beers. Reasonable prices, good music and friendly staff. 14 Rizospaton 26710 22022

Café Antico **14** Fashionable hangout and cool local crowd. Good views of street, comfortable seating, drinks, snacks and taped music. 7 Lithostrotos 26710 24581 Open until late

Phoenix Music Club **15** Popular locals' dance club bar with theme nights, indoor dance action and people watching in atmospheric garden bar. 2 George Vergotis Avenue, Platia Vallianou 69471 09737

Rumours **16** Lively music café-bar popular with locals. Platia Vallianou 26710 24524

⬥ *Kalamia beach is the nearest to Lassi*

Lassi & Lakythra
white beaches and quiet villages

Lassi is the name of the peninsula that separates the sheltered Koutavos lagoon, to the east, from the larger Gulf of Argostoli to the west. Since the arrival of tourism on Kefalonia, resort developments have spread along the west coast of the peninsula, from its northern tip, all the way down to the airport, about 11 km (7 miles) south.

Based in Lassi, you are never far from the island's capital, which is a 30-minute hike over the hill, or a 90-minute romantic stroll along the coastal road known as 'lovers' walk'. Lassi is ideally situated to make the most of the white-sand beaches of western Kefalonia (see map on page 38) and the enchanting village settlements south of Lakythra, only just opening up to tourism and set in olive groves and fruit orchards.

BEACHES
Kalamia
Closest to the centre of Lassi, Kalamia is set in a picturesque bay, with white cliffs backing a grey sand and shingle beach. Beach beds and umbrellas are for hire and there is a small bar. ➌ 2 km (1¼ miles) north of Lassi centre on the Fanari/Agostoli scenic road

Makris Yialos
This long stretch of golden sand is popular but big enough not to get impossibly crowded. It's perfect for families, with sheltered warm water, water sports' equipment and beach furniture for hire, one large beach café at the southern end and others above, overlooking the beach ➋ 800 m (880 yds) south of Lassi centre

Paliostafida
Just in front of the Mediterranee Hotel, this beach has grey sand and clear sea, beach beds and umbrellas for hire. ➊ Lassi centre

Platis Yialos

Golden sands and facilities that include showers and changing rooms.
❸ 1 km (½ mile) south of Lassi centre

Tourkopodaro

This peninsula of white beach has umbrellas and sunbeds mainly used by the White Rocks Hotel guests, but you can swim from neighbouring Platis Yialos and enjoy the views. The White Rocks Hotel is 1.5 km (1 mile) from Lassi centre.

RESTAURANTS & BARS

Aquarius Café Bar €€ Pleasant family-oriented café-bar that serves snacks, ice creams and the best cocktails in the resort, plus TV sports' coverage and 60s to current music. ❸ Central Lassi main street ❶ 26710 23556 ❷ Open 09.00–late

Chinese Dragon €€€ Authentic Chinese restaurant, magnificent views of the sunset and children's playground. ❸ Fanari Road ❶ 26710 22005

International € Traditional local grill dishes, pasta and delicious pizzas, with occasional musicians. ❸ Lassi village ❶ 26710 41388

La Gondola €€€ Italian restaurant with cosy ambience. Well-stocked bar and excellent range of Italian and Greek dishes. Major credit cards. Ideal venue for a special night out. ❸ Lassi main road ❶ 26710 25522

Monte Nero €€€ Try traditional mezedes and the huge variety of fresh fish; international dishes too. Local barrel wine and extensive wine list of over 90 well-known wines from all over Greece. Relaxing atmosphere, fine service, beautifully furnished. ❸ Lassi main road ❶ 26710 22646 ❷ Open for dinner only

The Olive Press €€ Flower-bedecked taverna with an old olive press outside. Welcoming atmosphere and open all day for breakfast, lunch and dinner. Live music nightly. ⓐ Minies, on road to the airport ☎ 6978 02263

Phaedra €€ Romantic open-air dining. Greek music, children's menu, fine selection of local wines which you can buy from the barrel to take home. Italian, Greek and English menu. Try the special Greek omelette. Major credit cards taken ⓐ Lassi main road ☎ 26710 26631

San Lorenzo €€ Set in unique courtyard-style setting and serving traditional Kefalonian and Italian dishes. Child-friendly menu and facilities. ⓐ Lassi centre, near to Makris Yialos ☎ 26710 25660

Sirtaki €€ Lively Greek taverna serving home-made local dishes, fresh fish and choice of bottled or barrelled wine in traditional décor. ⓐ Lassi main road ☎ 26710 23852

Sto Psito €€ Popular with locals and visitors alike, this friendly taverna serves up local specialities and barrel wine. ⓐ 2 km (1¼ miles) north of Lassi centre on Fanari/Argostoli scenic road ☎ 26710 25306 ⓛ Open for dinner only

SHOPPING

You can do all your shopping in Lassi's main road. Try **Veronica's** (☎ 26710 22191) for exquisite handmade jewellery, **Vagelati Supermarket** (☎ 26710 25590) for fresh fruit and vegetables, liquor and local wines, and **Lassi Supermarket** for a good range of provisions, holiday essentials, newspapers and magazines, etc.

EXCURSIONS
Corelli's Kefalonia Tour ★★★
Following in the footsteps of Captain Corelli, the central figure in *Captain Corelli's Mandolin*, this tour starts at the Italian War Memorial on the Lassi peninsula and continues to the small village of Kourkoumelata, rebuilt after the 1953 earthquake. You can see examples of pre-earthquake houses at Svoronata and visit Metaxata where Lord Byron stayed for four months. To the north is the 13th-century monastery of Aghios Andreas (St Andrew) and an ecclesiastical museum, and behind it, the now ruined fortress of Aghios Georgios (St George), with fine views across the south coast.

Cephalonia Paintball Park ★★
Paintball wars, suitable for teens and adults who enjoy hide 'n' seek strategy and getting splattered with paint. Set in an attractive parkland area with the Semeli Café-Wine Bar attached for reviving drinks and snacks. Ring to book a session. ❷ Keramies, near Peratata ❶ 26710 69220

Mount Ainos ★
The island's highest peak at 1628 m (5340 ft), covered in native fir trees once famous throughout Greece and used in building the palace at Knossos on Crete, is now a National Park, grazed by wild horses. A road goes part way up; thereafter walk to the summit along a rough track. ❷ 20 km (12 miles) east of Lassi

HOLIDAY READING
If you are looking for a good book to read whilst lazing on the beach, try *Captain Corelli's Mandolin*, by Louis de Bernières. This tells the story of the Italian invasion of the island in World War II and the events that led to the mass execution of 5000 Italian soldiers, known as the Kefalonia martyrs, on Hitler's direct orders. Gloomy as this sounds, the novel is full of lively humour and presents an authentic portrait of Greek island life.

Wine from Kefalonia ★★

Kefalonia produces some of the best white wine to be drunk anywhere in Greece. Much of it comes from the **Robola Producers' Co-operative**, in Ayia Gerassimos. The winery, behind the church, welcomes visitors. You can watch wine being produced or simply taste the wines.

ⓐ Ayia Gerassimos is 3 km (2 miles) south of Lassi

🕓 Factory open Mon–Fri, 07.00–15.00

🔺 *Makris Yialos beach (see page 45)*

○ *The church at Lixouri*

Lixouri
red sand beaches, chalk-white cliffs

Lixouri sits on the eastern side of the Gulf of Argostoli, looking across to the island's capital, which is only 30 minutes away by ferry (services half-hourly in high season from 07.30 to midnight). Despite being the island's second largest town, Lixouri is quiet and friendly, little touched by tourism and a good place to enjoy Grecian island life.

The statue of Andreas Laskaratos (1811–1901), situated by the ferry port, commemorates a poet who was also a noted wit. When the local priest excommunicated him for his irreverence, saying that his body would never rot unless he repented, Laskaratos rushed home to get his children's ragged clothes and hole-filled shoes, asking the priest to excommunicate them too. Beyond the ferry port is the main square with its shaded cafés. One of the few buildings to survive the earthquake of 1953 is now the **Museum**, with a small collection of religious icons (**ⓐ** Western side of the main road towards Hotel Palatino **ⓣ** 26710 91325 **ⓛ** Open Tues–Sun 08.30–13.30 **ⓘ** Admission charge).

BEACHES
Akrotiri
A small bay with a sweep of golden sand; no facilities but quiet and relaxing. **ⓐ** 10.5 km (6½ miles) south of Lixouri

Ammoudia (also known as Xi)
Red sand contrasts with chalk-white cliffs at this beach, which has a hotel and two tavernas. Sunbeds and umbrellas for hire. **ⓐ** 8 km (5 miles) south of Lixouri

Lepeda
Sandstone rocks carved into weird sculptures by the wind shelter this beach and provide a safe natural pool for children to bathe in. Sunbeds and parasols for hire. Taverna nearby. **ⓐ** 2 km (1¼ miles) south of Lixouri

Lixouri
Lixouri's nearest beach is a narrow strip of sand just south of the town centre, which is popular with families.

The cost of hiring sunbeds and beach umbrellas on the beaches of Kefalonia can mount up over a two-week holiday. Consider buying your own umbrella and mat from local shops, even if you leave them behind when you depart.

RESTAURANTS & BARS
Apolafsi €€ This is a friendly, family-run taverna where children are welcome. Try the fresh fish and specials of the day.
ⓐ 15 minutes' stroll south of Lixouri at Lepeda **ⓣ** 26710 91691

Canta Napoli € Traditional Greek and Italian goodies served in a lively ambience. Good wines. Families welcome. ⓐ Leoforos Rizospaston ❶ 26710 92238

Dionysos Musi Café € Good selection of coffees, teas, cocktails, snacks, sweets, ice creams etc. ⓐ Top left corner of the main square, Lixouri ❶ 26710 94208

Mella € Cool crowd, cool ambience and cool drinks. ⓐ Leoforos Rizospaston ❶ 26710 93435

Novita Restaurant €€ Spacious seating in the upstairs terrace overlooking the waterfront. Good wholesome dinners; the house speciality is fresh fish. Music bar. ⓐ Leoforos Rizospaston ❶ 26710 94251

Oasis € Cosy and comfortable pizzeria serving Greek and Italian fare, English breakfasts, ice creams, sweets and drinks. ⓐ Leoforos Rizospaston ❶ 26710 93384 ❷ Open until late

SHOPPING

Lixouri If you don't fancy the trip to Argostoli to shop for smart shoes and accessories, try the Lixouri branch of **Ertsos** in the town centre. ⓐ 4 Afon Livieraton ❶ 26710 94186

Patras The main shopping area in Patras is Aghios Nicolai, where you'll find plenty of shops, including a **Marks & Spencer**, pavement cafés and bars. Shops close at 14.00, so if you're a keen shopper leave lunch until last. Good buys in Patras at the **Achaia Clauss Winery** (❶ 2610 325051) include white wines such as Demestica and retsina. A guided tour of the winery and wine-tasting is offered daily 11.00–20.00 in summer, and 09.00–20.00 in winter. A litre bottle of the sweet red Mavrodaphne is very good value.

Sami
caves, ruins and beaches

Sami has the island's largest harbour and lies 22 km (14 miles) north east of Argostoli along the bay of the same name. According to Homer, ancient Sami stood outside the town to the north and the ruins are still visible on the hills next to the harbour. These days Kefalonia's main ferry port has a pleasant taverna-lined seafront and a fine pebble beach just north of the port.

RESTAURANTS & BARS

Captain Jimmy € Informal atmosphere, pool table, happy hour, seating on the waterfront. Try the delicious ice creams.
ⓐ Poseidon Street (waterfront) ❶ 26740 23059

Dolphins € Popular family run establishment for locals and visitors alike. Excellent local dishes of grills and fresh fish. Features local musicians and singers. ⓐ Sami (waterfront) ❶ 26740 22008

Faros €€ Home cooking in this friendly, family-run taverna. The moussaka is particularly good washed down with local wine.
ⓐ Sami waterfront ❶ 26740 23041

Karavomilos Tavern € Right on the seafront with a view of the duck-filled Karavomilos Lake. Try Kefalonian meat pie, lobster, kalamari or pasticcio. ⓐ Karavomilos ❶ 26740 22216

The Mermaid €€ Authentic Greek fare in quiet location at the back of town. ⓐ 300 m (984 ft) off the Karavomilos Road
❶ 26740 23057

Nea Sami €€ One of the first coffee shops in Sami, dating back to 1870. Excellent cakes and popular with the locals. Try a metrio (Greek coffee). ⓐ Sami waterfront ❶ 26740 22024

Skala
sand dunes and Roman ruins

Skala lies 31 km (19 miles) south east of Argostoli. Blessed with a long beach and low sand dunes, it is fast developing into a major tourist resort. The original village sat on a hill inland but, following the 1953 earthquake, was moved to its present site beside the sea. Modern Skala is laid back and easy going with fairly low-key nightlife, but the area is perfect for snorkelling and there are plenty of ruins to explore. The 2 km (1¼ mile) sand-and-shingle beach, fringed by pink and white oleander, is big enough never to be seriously overcrowded. Sunbeds and umbrellas can be hired by the day and there are plenty of water sports.

RESTAURANTS & BARS

Aeolos €€€ Smart beach restaurant. Try the seafood platter of lobster, crab, cod and prawns. Greek nights, including Greek dancing, are held weekly. Credit cards taken. ❸ Next door to Muses Hotel, Skala beach ❶ 26710 83561

The Cottage €€ Cosy open-air terrace to enjoy English breakfasts, pepper steaks, beer or cool white wines. ❸ Opposite the police station, Skala ❶ 26710 83238

Galera Restaurant/Bar €€ Corner location offering extensive wine list and Greek and international menu in romantic open-air setting. ❸ Opposite the police station, Skala ❶ 26710 83438

Green Paradise € Informal atmosphere. Good stop for basic English fare such as jacket potatoes and baked beans. ❸ Skala beach ❶ 26710 83334

Lucky House Restaurant € Beachside bar/restaurant serving fast food and Greek and Italian specialities. A good range of cocktails

⬥ *Skala beach is a perfect spot for sunbathing or snorkelling*

and spirits and daily menu which includes briam (mixed vegetables), swordfish, hamburgers, chicken wings and filling pancakes. ⓐ Skala beach ☎ 26710 83515 ◔ Happy hour 19.00–21.00

🍴 **La Luna** € Family-run restaurant serving tasty pizzas and grilled meat and chicken. ⓐ Main road, Skala ☎ 26710 83242

🍸 **Pikiona** €€ Up-market swimming pool complex which includes a bar and offers Guinness and Boddingtons on draught. Try the hydromassage and workouts in a garden setting. Music by DJs until late. ⓐ Skala beach ☎ 26710 83410 ⓦ www.pikiona.gr ◔ Open 10.00–03.00

🍴 **The Pines Restaurant** €€€ Corner location in pretty flower-bedecked restaurant giving good views of the street. Try the Greek or Italian specialities and barrel wine. ⓐ Skala ☎ 26710 83216 ◔ Open all day

🍴 **Siroco** €€ Open from breakfast time until late, this popular restaurant offers traditional charcoal-grilled meat and fish dishes. ⓐ Skala ☎ 26710 83229

Kefalonia excursions

BEACHES, VILLAGES & RUINS

Antisamos ★★

This white pebbled crescent-shaped beach backed by the most verdant of mountain backdrops is a unique opportunity to get away from it all. Take your own food since there is only one mobile food stall on the beach. The snorkelling is superb. Sunbeds and sun umbrellas for hire. It is a good idea to take your own food as there is only one mobile food stall and taverna. ❷ 4 km (2½ miles) east of Sami

Aghios Gerasimou Monastery ★★

This building is founded by the island's patron saint, whose mummified remains are kept in a beautiful silver casket on view during his festival days. Magnificent examples of Ionian icon/fresco paintings. Please dress modestly. ❷ Close to the Siroke Robola Co-op Winery, Valsamata

Assos ★★★

The unspoiled village of Assos clings to the island's western coast. The ruined Venetian fortress (1595) can be reached by footpaths from the small harbour. The protective walls once sheltered the villagers of Assos from the ravages of pirates. ❷ 22 km (14 miles) north of Lixouri

Drogarati Caves ★★★

The huge Drogarati Caves drip with stalactites and, with their excellent accoustics, are occasionally used for concerts. Note that you have to descend 120 steps to reach the entrance and that you will need to dress warmly. ❷ 3.5 km (2 miles) south west of Sami ◷ Open sunrise to sunset

Fiskardo ★★★

Perched on the tip of Kefalonia's northern finger, Fiskardo escaped serious damage during the 1953 earthquake, and is the island's prettiest village. Venetian-style houses cluster around the yacht-filled bay. It is also the most exclusive town on the island. ❷ 30 km (19 miles) north of Lixouri

Ithaka ★★★

One of the most popular trips from Sami is the 30-minute ferry to neighbouring Ithaka. Numerous temples and ruins on the island are linked with Odysseus, including the capital Vathy, with its Venetian fortresses and the stalactite-hung Cave of the Nymphs, 2 km (1¼ miles) to the west.

Melissani Lake and Cave ★★★

The Melissani Cave was used as a temple in pre-Christian times by worshippers of the god Pan. Visitors explore the cave by boat, lit from above by a hole in the cave roof. ➋ 4 km (2½ miles) north west of Sami

Myrtos Beach ★★★

Spectacular Myrtos (Mirtos) is everybody's idea of the perfect beach, with its half-moon of silver shingle sliding into the shallows of an azure-blue sea. Sunbeds and umbrellas for hire. ➋ 18 km (11 miles) north of Lixouri

Neighbouring islands ★★★

Lefkas (see page 14) and Zante (see page 58) are both within easy reach of Kefalonia, with daily ferry services from Fiskardo and Pessada.

Patras ★

Patras is the main port for ferries to Italy and a number of Greek islands. The central area of the old town is a shopper's paradise and other attractions include a 6th-century AD fortress and a visit to the Achaia Clauss winery. The daily ferry from Sami, takes 2½ hours.

Poros ★★

Poros has direct ferry links to Kilini on the mainland. Warm turquoise waters and delightful fish tavernas ➋ 13 km (8 miles) north of Skala

Ruins of the Temple of Apollo ★

These 7th-century BC ruins were discovered next to the tiny church of Aghios Georgios. The waters here are ideal for snorkelling.
➋ Porto Skala, 2 km (1¼ miles) north of Skala

THE ISLAND OF ZANTE

N

| 0 | 5 km | 10 km |
| 0 | | 6 miles |

Kianou Caves

SKINARI
AGHIOS
NICOLAOS

Navagio
(Smuggler's
Cove)

VOLIMES

ALYKES

IONIAN SEA

ANAFONITRIA

KATASTARI

ALYKANAS

PORTO
VROMI

Pigadakia

ANO
GERAKARI

TRAGAKI

Tsilivi

756m

KAMPI

ZANTE

ZANTE TOWN

GALAROU

MACHERADO

ARGASSI

KALAMAKI

AGHIOS
LEONTAS

Mt.
Skopos
470 m

LAGANAS

VASSILIKOS

LITHAKIA

Laganas/
Turtle Bay

PELUZO

BEACHES

AGALAS

LIMNI
KERIOU

MARATHONISI

Caves

KERI

MARATHIA

1 AGHIOS NIKOLAOS

2 AMBOULLA

3 BANANA
BEACH

4 BOUKA

5 GERAKAS

6 PLANOS

7 PORTO ROMA

Zante Town
'Flower of the Levant'

You would not know that the capital of Zante had been destroyed by an earthquake in 1953, so well has the town been rebuilt in a style that tries to recapture the former elegance of a town once known as the 'Flower of the Levant'. Ruled by Venice for over 300 years, the streets of Zante are a refreshing blend of Grecian and Venetian styles, with traditional arcades running round the two main squares and along Alexandrou Roma, the main shopping street, and providing welcome shade from the sun.

Zante's busy harbour is alive with craft of all kinds: fishing boats unloading their catch, inter-island ferries, sleek yachts and luxurious cruise ships. To the south of the harbour stands the church of Aghios Dionysios (St Dennis), one of the few buildings to survive the earthquake, with a tall campanile (bell tower) modelled on the one in St Mark's Square in Venice. Local people attribute the survival of the church to the protection of St Dennis, whose mummified body lies inside in a silver coffin.

On the craggy hilltop above the town there are the ruins of the ancient Venetian kastro, or fortress, where townspeople sheltered from piratical raids. More like a miniature town than a castle, the kastro offers superb views from its walls. Passing through gateways carved with the lion of St Mark, symbol of Venice, you can explore the remains of old chapels, warehouses and barrack buildings. ◕ Open 08.00–19.30 (summer); 08.00–14.00 (winter) ❶ Admission charge

AGHIOS DIONYSIOS
Aghios Dionysios (St Dennis) is the island's patron saint and his feast day is celebrated on 24 August. On this day, the saint is given a new pair of slippers, because it is believed that he wears out the old ones wandering around the island doing good deeds.

NAUTICAL MUSEUM

DIONISSIOU ROMA

FILIKON

N. KOLIVA

✝ CATHEDRAL

MUSEUM OF SOLOMOS
PL. AG. MARKOU
MAIOU ST.

ARCHAEOLOGICAL MUSEUM

✝ PLATIA SOLOMOU

TOWN HALL ℹ️

N. KOLIVA

FOSKOLOU ST.

LOMBARDOU

ZANTE

KOLMOUSI

ALEXANDROU ROMA ST.

✝

FILITA

PLATIA AG. LOUKA

LIGHTHOU

Zante Harbour

Marina

AGIOU DIONISSIOU

AGIOU LAZAROU

KALVOU

✝

MUSEUM OF AGHIOS DIONYSIOS

THINGS TO SEE & DO
Archaeological and Neo-Byzantine Museum ★★
Photographs and scale models detail the appearance of Zante Town before the 1953 earthquake. There is also an outstanding collection of frescos and religious paintings rescued from churches all over the island.
🅐 Platia Solomou 🕿 26950 42714 🕒 Open Tues–Sun 09.00–14.00
Admission charge

Museum of Solomos and Notable Zakynthians ★★
This small museum contains the tomb of the local poet, Dionysios Solomos (1798–1857), whose great claim to fame is that he wrote the words to the Greek national anthem, the Hymn to Freedom. Exhibits cover the life of Solomos and other prominent citizens of Zante.
🅐 Platia Ag Markou 🕿 26950 48982 🕒 Open Tues–Sun 09.00–14.00
ⓘ Admission charge

Nautical Museum ★
Contains exhibits of the nautical history of Greece – the only museum in Greece to portray the country's nautical history from 1700BC to the present day. See the display of ships that took part in the Greek Revolution of 1821. 🅐 Fillikon Street near Strani Hill 🕿 26950 28249
🕒 Open Mon–Sun 09.30–14.30 and 18.30–22.30 ⓘ Admission charge

> ## SHOPPING
> The two main shopping streets in Zante are Alexandrou Roma Street and Maiou Street, leading into the main square, Agiou Markou, with its tree-shaded cafés. Tourist shops sell ceramic turtles and the local specialities, *mandoláto* (white honey-flavoured nougat with almonds) and *pustéli* (bars made of honey and sesame seeds).

RESTAURANTS (see map on page 60)

Arekia €€ ❶ Considered by many to be the island's best traditional taverna and often crowded with locals. Local folk song performances from 22.00. ⓐ Dionissiou Roma ☎ 26950 26346

Arestis Piano Bar/Restaurant €€€ ❷ Overlooking the sea, this taverna/restaurant serves international fare and is tastefully furnished. Dress up and enjoy the views. ⓐ Akrotiri ☎ 26950 27379

Big Boy's No 5 Express € ❸ Greek-style hamburgers, but try the chopped steak sandwich or country-style sandwich. Special kids' meals too. ⓐ Platia Solomou ☎ 26950 43018

Café San Marco € ❹ Intimate and cosy. Great for people-watching and right beside the Solomos Museum. ⓐ 9 Platia Ag Markou ☎ 26950 28832 ⏰ Open until late

Corner Restaurant €€ ❺ Pizzeria, grills and traditional Greek food, tables outside or in. Friendly service. ⓐ 10 Platia Ag Markou ☎ 26950 42654

Gregoris €€ ❻ Good selection of Greek fast food with a lively atmosphere and tables outside on the square ⓐ Platia Ag Markou ☎ 26950 44701

Kokkinos Vrahos €€€ ❼ Big, bold and new and overlooking Platia Solomou. Italian and Greek dishes, drinks, ice creams. Perfect location for evening people-watching in the square. ⓐ Platia Solomou ☎ 26950 42005 ⏰ Open until 04.00

Komis €€ ❽ Opposite the church of Aghios Dionysios, this fish taverna serves a wide-ranging menu of freshly caught fish and grills. Try swordfish or grilled kalamari in traditional Greek atmosphere. ⓐ Platia Agiou Dionysios ☎ 26950 26915

⏵ *Zante Town's elegant buildings*

Panorama €€€ ❾ Up-market venue with sweeping views over Zante in the nearby hamlet of Bokhali. Serves local dishes as well as international food. Booking advised. ⓐ Bokhali ❶ 26950 28862

Porto € ❿ Bar-snacks on the pier. Good place to watch the inter-island ferries whilst sipping an ouzo. ⏱ Open until late

Porto Fino Cafe € ⓫ Very relaxing by the sea. Ideal for snacks, coffee and ice creams. ⓐ On the Kryoneri Road, further down from the Green Boat

Spitiko €€ ⓬ Traditional Greek and local dishes, popular with locals too. Good local wines. ⓐ Platia Ag Markou ❶ 26950 23722

Venetziana International €€€ ⓭ Enjoy the cool night air. Italian, Greek and international cuisine. ⓐ Platia Ag Markou ❶ 26950 23722

Argassi
on the slopes of Mount Skopos

Argassi is a family resort with a fine beach on the doorstep, 1 km (½ mile) in length and offering a wide variety of water sports. The town offers plenty of nightlife opportunities and is only a short distance from the capital, Zante Town (see page 59).

Argassi is an excellent base for exploring Mount Skopos, the highest point on the island rising to 470 m (1540 ft) and a good place to look for wild orchids and rare butterflies. The name of this mountain means 'Look-out' and you will understand why if you travel to the summit: the views take in the whole of the island and the nearby Peloponnese, as well as the Bay of Navarino in between, site of a major naval battle in 1827.

RESTAURANTS

Big Boys € Greek fast-food chain, eat in or take away, serving gyros, souvlaki, burgers, sandwiches. ❸ Argassi centre ❶ 26950 27562

Carrissimo €€ Traditional Greek and international food, including the local Zakynthian beef stew. Friendly staff and shaded terrace. ❸ Argassi coast road ❶ 26950 45669

Courser €€ Excellent Chinese restaurant in the heart of the resort. Extensive menu, making good use of the fresh local ingredients. ❸ Near Magic Mushroom junction ❶ 26950 42311

Edem €€ The most authentically Greek of all the resort's restaurants, with friendly staff and outdoor terrace. ❸ Argassi coast road ❶ 26950 42242

Enigma €€ On the edge of the resort, this is a relaxing taverna away from the main throng, serving excellent vegetable lasagne, pizzas and beef stroganoff. ❸ Argassi coast road, near the church

Ilision €€€ This restaurant, away from the centre, has a good reputation for its excellent menu, including Greek specialities and vegetarian. ❸ One block inland from Magic Mushroom jct ❶ 26950 42181

 Phoenix € Serves great pizzas, plus pasta and traditional Greek dishes. ❸ Argassi coast road ❶ 26950 49062

 Stars €€ Popular Greek taverna, on the main street but away from the main throng. ❸ Argassi coast road, opposite the bank ❶ 26950 42875

 Symposion €€€ Seafront restaurant in the outskirts of the resort, with live piano music and romantic ambience. Italian and Greek food. ❸ Argassi coast road, towards Zante Town ❶ 26950 43731

Venetziana €€ Try rabbit Zakynthos-style at this Greek restaurant, set back from the main road. Live Greek music at night. ❸ Five-minute walk inland from the Magic Mushroom ❶ 26950 26230

NIGHTLIFE
The Magic Mushroom Club Located in the centre of the resort, where most of the bars and nightspots are to be found, this club is used as a guide for directing people around the resort and to the other clubs:

Avalon Disco plus bar with large screen video/TV showing most major sporting events.

Factory Popular dance music (English DJ) and karaoke, plus live sport on TV on Saturdays. ❶ 26950 65012

Kiss Good music and party atmosphere.

Jungle Pub at the front and disco at rear; dance acts liven up the evening.

Magic Mushroom Swimming pool, pub and dancing club combined.

Red Lion Bar Popular bar serving 11 draught beers, more than 50 bottled beers, cocktails and a wide range of snacks. Fun, music and TV sports bar. Weekly programme of pub competitions and live music nights – Irish, rock, Greek. ❸ Argassi main road (opposite Hotel Mimoza) ❶ 26950 43815

Laganas
home of the loggerhead turtle

Laganas has possibly the finest beach on Zante, a 4 km (2½ mile) sweep of golden sand, gently shelving into a jewel-like sea as warm as bath water. This bay is also the nesting area for around 80 per cent of the Mediterranean's population of the Loggerhead Turtle, and conservation measures now in place ensure that there is no danger to the turtles from speed boats and jet skis. This makes for a relatively quiet life on the beach, though the nightlife is the liveliest on Zante.

◆ Seafood is a local speciality

THINGS TO SEE & DO
Laganas Go-Kart & Crazy Golf ★★
Open all day, this go-karting centre with crazy golf, bar, cafeteria and fruit machines, provides fun for all the family. ❸ Zakinthos Road at the junction with Kalamaki Road

---

EGGS IN THE SAND
The breeding season for the shy loggerhead turtle coincides with the main holiday season. During July and August, the females come ashore to lay their eggs about 50 cm (20 inches) below the surface. The eggs are insulated by the warm sand, and the baby turtles hatch some eight weeks later, crawling towards the bright moonlit sea. **Archelon**, an organisation set up to save the Loggerhead Turtles, takes volunteers to work on the island (❶ 21052 31342 Ⓦ www.archelon.gr).

BEACHES
Laganas Bay
The ban on water sports imposed to protect the loggerhead turtles means that this is a quiet family beach, perfect for children because of the warm shallow water and fine sand, with plenty of room for everyone: the stretches of beach nearest the resort can be busy, but you do not have to walk far to find a less crowded spot. Loungers for hire; tavernas nearby.

RESTAURANTS

Akropolis €€ Beautiful countryside setting, surrounded by olive groves. Do not miss the garlic prawns. ⓐ Pandokratoras Road, Laganas ❶ 26950 51168

La Bella Napoli €€ Also known as the 'Italian' restaurant, the name says it all: excellent pizza and pasta, plus more substantial dishes, such as grilled steak. ⓐ Pandokratoras Road, Laganas

Cozy Corner € Good choice for fast food, including hamburgers, pizzas and spit-roast lamb in pitta bread. ⓐ Zakinthos Road, Laganas ❶ 26950 51864

Fatsos € Eat as much as you like salads, grills and hamburgers at this value for money eaterie. ⓐ Kalamaki Road ❶ 26950 52255 ❶ Open until late

Giorgio's €€€ Lively restaurant run by Greek-Canadian family, with American and oriental dishes on the extensive menu, including stir fries, steaks and ribs. ⓐ Opposite Hotel Alexander, Kalamaki Road ❶ 26950 52255

I Fratelli €€€ This well-frequented restaurant provides bay vista seating and offers Mediterranean and local cuisine. ⓐ On the beach road ❶ 26950 51178

Ionian Sea €€€ Enjoy mixed seafood platters or lamb kleftiko in the garden of this friendly taverna. ⓐ Kalamaki Road
ⓣ 26950 51797

Jacket Potato Place € Just what you need for a cheap and filling lunch: jacket potatoes with scores of different fillings.
ⓐ Zakinthos Road, Laganas ⓣ 26950 51195

Paradise €€ This elegant but reasonably priced townhouse restaurant specialises in traditional lamb and chicken dishes, as well as fresh fish, such as sea bass. ⓐ Zakinthos Road near the Paradise Apartments ⓣ 26950 52516

Prince of India & Ruby Chinese €€€ The place to try Chinese or Indian cuisine. Balti dishes and take-away. ⓐ Kalamaki Road
ⓣ 26950 52696 ⓛ Open for dinner only, 16.00–01.00

Romio's €€ Opened in 2002, this restaurant and pizzeria is located one block back from the seafront. Special menu for kids.
ⓐ Laganas ⓣ 26950 51900

Sarakina €€€ Live Greek music and dancing makes a meal here more of an occasion. Set in the hills, ten minutes from the centre (with free transport available), with good views over the nearby Mansion ruins and the hills. ⓐ Sarakina Mansions ⓣ 26950 51606

Taj Mahal €€ As a change from Greek food, why not try this Indian restaurant specialising in chicken tikka massala, seafood and meat curries and the Taj Mahal Special Biryani. ⓐ Kalamaki Road
ⓣ 26950 51783

Venetziana €€ Popular venue for international and Greek fare at good value. Extensive menu and friendly service. ⓐ Zakinthos Road, Laganas ⓣ 26950 51698

NIGHTLIFE

The hub of Laganas' nightlife is centred on the **Zakinthos Road** just inland from the beach, with a wide choice of bars, fun clubs and lots of party people. The music is mainly HipHop, R&B and Dance Music.

La Bamba Comfortable colonial-style karaoke bar.

Cherry Bay Beach Bar Cocktail bar and nightclub situated right on the beach, with lively staff and a *Baywatch* theme.

Cocktails and Dreams Trendy young nightspot above Planet Zante based on the bar from the film *Cocktail* and serving a mix of 50 cocktails with dance music.

Ghetto Club Classy bar serving excellent cocktails.

Nikos Cocktails Cocktails and live TV coverage of big sporting events.

Rescue One of the resort's two largest dance clubs (see Zero's); free entry with theme nights; live dance groups and singers. 🕐 Open 18.30–04.00 weekdays and until 06.00 Fri and Sat

Saloon Happy hour prices to 21.30, then a musical quiz most nights, leading into a night of rock and pop classics. Special party nights.

Waikiki A noisy bar-cum-club – cool hangout for night owls.
🕐 Open until late

Bad Boys R'n'B Not original R'n'B as in Eric Clapton style, but Beyonce, Black Eyed Peas, etc. A good atmosphere to party in.

Zero's The alternative to Rescue if you are looking for a big dance club playing house/dance/party music. Special theme nights.
🕐 Open weekdays 18.30–04.00, Fri and Sat 18.30–06.00

ZANTE

The name of Zante is said to derive from the wild hyacinths that still grow on this lush green island, which the Venetians nick-named the 'Flower of the Levant'. The luxuriant landscape is planted with orange and olive groves, almond orchards and vine-yards, producing tiny sweet grapes for drying and turning into succulent raisins.

Kalamaki
golden sands and offshore islands

Kalamaki is a relaxed family resort whose beach is an extension of that at Laganas, offering the same clean golden sands and crystal clear waters.

The beach is five minutes from the resort centre and is relatively quiet, due to nesting Loggerhead Turtles. There are showers, and pedalos, canoes, umbrellas and sunbeds for hire. Because of the nesting turtles, visitors to the beach are asked not to stick umbrellas in the sand in the marked nesting zones, or to dig up the turtle eggs. Use of the beach is banned during the hours of darkness. ❶ Baby turtles should never be handled

THINGS TO SEE & DO
Horse riding ★★
Kids can spend a morning pony riding in the countryside. Details from the **Riding Centre**, Kalamaki. ❶ 6976 44029

Mini Golf ★★★
There's fun for all ages to be had at the 18-hole **Kalamaki Mini Golf**. Golf balls and clubs are provided and refreshments and snacks are available. ❷ In the centre of Kalamaki resort ❸ Open April–Oct 10.00–01.00

RESTAURANTS & BARS
🍴 **Buon Amici** €€ Popular Italian restaurant with indoor air-conditioned seating area and terrace. Excellent range of Greek and Italian wines. ❷ Zakinthos Road ❶ 26950 22915

🍴 **Merlis** €€ Lively restaurant serving Greek and European food; large and varied mezedes (a banquet made up of many different dishes). ❷ Zakinthos Road ❶ 26950 45003

🍴 **Michaelos** €€ Family-run taverna; friendly and happy to cook special dishes on request. ❷ Zakinthos Road ❶ 26950 48080

Pavlos €€€ Typical Greek taverna with children's play area. Try the oven-roasted lamb or – if you are vegetarian – the special vegetable platters. ⓐ Zakinthos Road ⓣ 26950 45285

Pelouzo Taverna €€ Varied English and Greek menus in this taverna attached to Crystal Beach Hotel. Facilities such as the swimming pool overlooking the seafront are open to non-residents. Try the daily specials from bean soup to steak Diane. ⓐ Seafront ⓣ 26950 42774

Sofias €€ Local and traditional Greek cuisine, meat and fish grills. ⓐ Near Kalamaki centre ⓣ 69778 60732

Sugar Reef € Lively pizzeria and cocktail bar with Australian staff. ⓐ Laganas Road ⓣ 26950 22452

▲ Kalamaki beach

Taverna Zepos €€ Across the road from Crystal Beach Hotel, this terraced garden area offers great mezedes and traditional cooking. ⓐ Seafront ⓣ 26950 27698

NIGHTLIFE

Al'Sandros Centrally located, friendly bar with pool table and friendly staff. ⓐ Zakinthos Road

Cave Bar Stylish traditional Greek bar located in a cave with panoramic views. ⓐ Look out for the sign on the hill

Down Under Newly opened bar with occasional live music and karaoke evenings, all with an Aussie flavour and fun bar staff. ⓐ Vyzadio Road

Vassilikos
peninsular paradise

Vassilikos is situated on the south-eastern tip of Zante, on the peninsula formed by the mountain range that separates this resort from those at Kalamaki and Argassi. Arguably the prettiest part of the island, the peninsula offers a succession of coves and beaches backed by lush pines.

Just one road links the small villages that make up the Vassilikos peninsula along which traditional tavernas and restaurants are strung. Car hire is essential to explore.

Looking for a picnic beach? There are so many to choose from, so don't stop at the first one you see but drive to Gerakas at the end of the peninsula and work your way back to explore them all. That way you won't find the best beach on the last day!

BEACHES
Aghios Nikolaos
Water sports facilities – and a bar sat on top of a rocky outcrop in the middle of the beach – attract visitors to this sandy spot, 3km (2 miles) south of Vassilikos. There is also a large modern hotel, with swimming pool and restaurants, open to non-residents.

Banana Beach
Nobody seems to know how this beach got its name, but Banana Beach is a popular spot just south of Vassilikos, with bars and water sports facilities.

SHOPPING

The **Fruit Market** is the best place to shop for home-grown fruit and veg. **Mais Supermarket** sells newspapers, beach goods, delicatessen foods, jewellery and ceramics.

⬤ *Aghios Nikolaos offers a stunning spot for picnics*

Gerakas

Some say that this beach is the best in the Ionian Islands; it certainly has all the ingredients for a long lazy day by the sea: golden sand, warm shallow waters and shelter from the wind provided by sandy cliffs. There are two tavernas and a snack bar but no water sports, because of the breeding turtles.

Porto Roma

Small sheltered cove with a sand and pebble beach, plus bar and taverna 5 km (3 miles) south of Vassilikos.

RESTAURANTS

Agnadi €€ Terraced taverna with panoramic views over the coast. Greek cooking, relaxing atmosphere and family-run.
ⓐ Xirokastello, Vassilikos ☏ 26950 35337

Babis € Authentic taverna with pretty terrace for outdoor dining.
ⓐ Ano Vassilikos village

Coffee House € Drop in for coffee, ouzo or cocktails at this friendly coffee house; try the local tsikoudia, a clear, schnapps-like drink. ⓐ Ano Vassilikos

Dioscuri €€ If you don't want to go the whole hog, try the mezedes of grilled pepper, aubergines, aubergine salad and tara-masalata. Family cooking in pleasant garden setting. ⓐ Ano Vassilikos village opposite O Gallos ☏ 26950 35316

Galini €€ Family-run taverna, fresh fish, grills, choice dishes, plenty of parking. You can stroll in the nearby forest, and there is a play area for the children. ⓐ South of Vassilikos village ☏ 26950 35231

🔺 *Banana Beach*

O Gallos €€ Excellent French/Greek restaurant with a singing and bouzouki-playing owner. ⓐ Ano Vassilikos village ⓣ 26950 35460

Giovanni €€ Try rabbit if you want to be adventurous or the kokinisto beef stew. ⓐ Ano Vassilikos village ⓣ 26950 35471

Kostas Brothers €€ Flower-filled garden and terrace. Regular performances of traditional songs to guitar and mandolin accompaniment. Try the delicious pork roast, stuffed with garlic and herbs. ⓐ Ano Vassilikos village ⓣ 26950 35347

Lithies € Meaning 'stones', Lithies serves a good range of local dishes (village-style chicken, Zakinthian beef stew) plus fresh fish. ⓐ Ano Vassilikos village ⓣ 26950 35290

Mais Coffee Shop € Alfresco meals. No menu but ask for the butter beans in tomato sauce, tzatziki and special meatballs. Supermarket next door sells basics. ⓐ Ano Vassilikos main road ⓣ 26950 35232

To Steki €€ Greek taverna serving traditional meals on beautiful bougainvillaea-clad terrace. Rooms to rent in same complex. Friendly service. ⓐ Xirokastello, Vassilikos ⓣ 26950 35205

Triodi €€ Some unusual offerings of mezedes and grills at this Greek taverna on the way to Gerakas beach. ⓐ Gerakas–Vasilikos Road ⓣ 26950 35215

NIGHTLIFE

Logos Enjoy generous cocktails in the tree-shaded garden. Air-conditioned dance floor and regular themed parties. ⓐ Ano Vassilikos ⓣ 26950 35296

Alykes & Alykanas
golden beaches and shallow waters

Just 15km (9 miles) from Zante Town on the north-east coast, Alykes (pronounced 'Al-lick-ess') and Alykanas (pronounced 'Al-lick-ah-nas') are ideal family resorts occupying 3km (2 miles) of golden sand which shelve gently into crystal-clear, shallow waters.

THINGS TO SEE & DO
The Vertzagio Popular Art Museum ★★
Newly opened and well signposted from Alykes, this museum contains a fascinating collection of rare farming artefacts from the mid-19th century. See the flourmill, olive press, traditional crafts and antique bedroom full of old lamps and furniture with descriptions annotated in English. Children will love the gentle donkeys and goats that roam in the courtyard. ❸ Pigadakia ❶ 26950 83670 ❻ Open 09.00–18.00 ❶ Admission charge

RESTAURANTS

Anatolikos Greek Taverna €€ Friendly, rustic taverna overlooking the sea with an extensive menu of Greek, Italian and English food. ❸ Alykes main road ❶ 26950 83158

Astoria Restaurant €€ Welcoming restaurant attached to waterfront hotel of the same name. Try the hearty English breakfasts or pancakes with maple syrup. ❸ Alykes seafront ❶ 26950 83533

Dionysos €€ Try saganaki or feta cheese as a starter followed by tasty keftedes (meat balls) for a traditional Greek meal and wash it down with the local wine at this taverna. ❸ Alykanas ❶ 26950 83954

Montes €€ Friendly, family run pizzeria and taverna. ❸ Alykes ❶ 26950 83100 ❾ www.montes.gr ❻ Open breakfast time until late

Oasis Greek Restaurant €€ This taverna serves Greek, Italian and English food and the café-bar has satellite TV which shows the latest sporting events. ⓐ Alykanas ⓣ 26950 83393

Olympic €€ Enjoy everything from pizzas to tasty Greek cooking and Indian specialities in the ambience of this restaurant where decorative Canadian number plates and a phone booth that doubles as a fridge reflect the taste of the Canadian-Greek owner, Bobby Leftakis. ⓐ Alykes main road ⓣ 26950 83507

Paporo €€ Try an enticing range of cocktails before dinner and enjoy the fabulous views of the sunset at this welcoming restaurant. ⓐ Alykes main road ⓣ 26950 83950 ⓦ www.paporo.gr ⓛ Open 09.00–late

Paradosiako €€ This traditional Greek taverna nestles beneath huge shady trees and offers a good selection of home cooking and local wine. ⓐ Alykanas–Zante Road ⓣ 26950 83412

Taj Mahal € Delicious selection of Chinese and Indian food. On the Katastari Road, north from ⓐ Alykes ⓣ 26950 83957

Taverna Kaki Raxi € For typical and traditional Greek meals in a village atmosphere. Families welcome. ⓐ Pigadakia ⓣ 26950 83670

NIGHTLIFE

Palm Tree Bar 1 and 2 Relax by day at the beachside bar over breakfast, snacks, ice creams and drinks and come night enjoy a cocktail, watch league matches on TV or dance until 03.00 in the bar on the main road. ⓐ Alykes main road opposite Montes Restaurant

Relax Bar Covered terrace, friendly service and lots of snacks, grills and pizzas at this corner venue in Alykes with good views of the main street. ⓐ Alykanas–Zante Road ⓣ 26950 83127

● Tsilivi is full of vineyards and orchards

Tsilivi
pretty beaches and plenty of fun

Tsilivi (pronounced 'Sill-ivi') is just 5 km (3 miles) north of Zante Town and 9 km (5½ miles) from the airport, on the north-east coast of Zante. The long safe beach of soft sand and clear waters has plenty to offer in the way of water sports. The huge bay attracts windsurfers and water-skiers and offers activities such as paragliding, pedalo and ringo rides. In spite of plenty of shops, bars, tavernas and restaurants, Tsilivi's traditional charm still attracts young couples and families. To the west of Tsilivi are more uncrowded beaches via short access roads through delightful orchards and vineyards.

If you learn only two words of Greek, make them *yia sou*. This is an all-purpose greeting which means not only 'hello' but also 'cheers' when having a drink. Greeks will reply *stin igia sas* ('to your health'), but don't be offended when they walk away because *yia sou* also means 'goodbye'.

BEACHES
Amboulla
Golden sands, quiet and with just a few tavernas 1 km (½ mile) to the west of Bouka beach. Dive centre on the beach provides water sports.

SHOPPING
The **Tom & John Centre** is a one-stop shopping complex in the centre of Tsilivi which includes exchange facilities, post office, public telephone, travel agency, supermarket, car hire, swimming pool and a bar for cool drinks and snacks.
🅐 Tsilivi centre ☎ 26950 42684

Bouka

Small, clean and sandy beach with shallow water which is not crowded.

Planos

Planos, an extension of Tsilivi, has several tavernas and shops. Umbrellas and parasols can be hired for the day.

RESTAURANTS

Abracadabra € Terraced setting on a grassy slope with views of Cape Gaidaros to the west. Serves snacks, drinks and ice creams and has a typical Greek atmosphere. ⓐ Bouka beach ❶ 26950 45050

Ariadne €€ A traditional Greek taverna serving typical local dishes. ⓐ Tsilivi centre ❶ 26950 43750

The Balcony of Zante € Snack bar serving a variety of Greek mezedes. Spectacular views across Tsilivi beach from this hillside location to the east of Tsilivi. ⓐ Tsilivi ❶ 26950 28638 ❷ Open until late

Chicken Texas € Try grilled chicken, pitta souvlaki or the village sausage at this friendly garden restaurant or tuck into a light salad or ice cream. ⓐ Tsilivi centre ❶ 26950 42332

La Fioro €€ Good pizzeria with an ample, covered terrace. ❶ 26950 27086

Iakinthos €€ Right on the beach, this complex has a bar and swimming pool. The restaurant serves a wide range of snacks and Greek and international fare. ⓐ Tsilivi seafront ❶ 26950 49028

O Kalofagas €€ Just inland from Amboulla beach on the main road, this well-established fish taverna serves excellent kalamari, swordfish and octopus. Good wine and Greek music. ⓐ 3 km (2 miles) west of Tsilivi ❶ 26950 62634

Limanaki €€ This is a popular fish taverna on the beach, which also serves English and international food. 🅐 Tsilivi Planos
🕐 26950 44740

Mango Beach Bar € Snacks, barbecues and drinks in this beachside bar which also hires sunbeds. Also has a play area for children. 🅐 Tsilivi centre 🕐 093 2817201 (mobile)

Moby Dick € Children's menu, English breakfasts, fish fingers and chips plus Greek food in this small eaterie just across the road from Iakinthos. 🅐 Tsilivi seafront 🕒 Open until late

The Old Vineyard €€ Typical open-air taverna near the beach offering traditional Greek fare and wine from the barrel.
🅐 Bouka beach

Pieros Restaurant €€ Authentic Greek and international meals served in typical Zakyithian surroundings in this restaurant, which is popular with locals. Children are welcome. 🅐 Tsilivi centre
🕐 26950 27046

Popeye's €€ Popular restaurant and pizzeria with a large terrace overlooking the main square. Also serves a full English breakfast.
🅐 Tsilivi 🕐 26950 41759 🌐 www.popeyestsilivi.com

Trenta Nova €€ Greek cuisine, pizza and snacks served in this outdoor snack bar. 🅐 Tsilivi centre 🕐 26950 22490 🕒 Open 09.00 until the last customer leaves!

NIGHTLIFE

Enigma Discover the cream of clubbing and an array of cocktails at this cool night venue. 🅐 Tsilivi centre
Planet Bar Drink your cocktails by the pool. 🕒 Open until 06.00 in high season

Zante excursions
caves, crafts and sunsets

BOAT TOURS

The **Kianou Caves**, at the northern tip of the island, are only accessible by boat. Kianou means 'blue' and you will understand why when you dip into the translucent blue waters that fill these magical sea grottos. Boat trips from the major resorts also visit **Smugglers' Cove** (also known as Shipwreck Cove or Navagio), named after a cargo ship – said to have come to grief on a smuggling mission – that lies half-buried in the sands beneath the sheer cliffs. Tour boats drop anchor here to allow passengers to enjoy views of the dazzling white cliffs and to take a dip in the clear waters.

Only follow the signs from Anafonitria turning left at Georges Tavern if you want to take a boat trip to The Wreck from Port Vromi. If you're driving yourself and want a bird's-eye view from the cliffs, then start from **Volimes** and drive south for 2.5 km (1½ miles) where an access road on the right marked 'The Wreck' leads to Navagio. A platform here enables you to take that unforgettable picture-postcard view.

MONASTERIES & CRAFTS

The traditional handicraft village of Volimes, in the north of Zante, is the place to browse for rugs, lace, carpets, table-linen and all sorts of crafts at bargain prices. Nearby is the Anafonitrias monastery, where Aghios Dionysios, the patron saint of the island, spent his final years as abbot. Besides relics of the saint, the monastery has 15th-century icons and 17th-century frescos.

Towards the end of the day, head for Kampi, on the island's west coast. Why? For spectacular cliff-edge views of the sun going down over the Ionian Sea. The village has a small folk museum, but the big draw, without doubt, is a ringside seat in one of the two tavernas perched 300 m (985 ft) above the sea.

🔺 *Discover 15th-century icons at Zante*

THE SOUTHERN TIP

The village of Keri escaped the worst effects of the 1953 earthquake and some fine old Venetian-style buildings have survived. A path from the village goes to the lighthouse at the southernmost tip of the island, with cliffs eroded into sculptural shapes by the wind and waves. Inland, **Macherado** has the most ornate Greek Orthodox church on the island. **Aghia Mavra** has a richly decorated interior and Venetian-style bell tower.

RESTAURANTS

Anemomylos €€ Panoramic views over the coast and pine-clothed countryside from this modern restaurant which serves Greek and English food, snacks and drinks. ⓐ Keri ☎ 26950 51750

Dennis Taverna €€ Off the tourist track and very popular with locals. Go for rabbit, chicken or grilled meats. ⓐ On the Keri Road, junction with Lithakia ☎ 26950 51387

To Fanari Taverna €€ Savour the delicious home-made wine and home-style cooking in romantic clifftop location. ⓐ 1 km (½ mile) after Keri village ☎ 26950 43384

La Grotta €€ Bustling taverna right next to the viewpoint at Navagio. Popular stop with coach parties. Huge menu which includes rather special dolmades (stuffed vine leaves) and scrumptious tiropitta (cheese pastries). ⓐ Navagio ☎ 26950 31224

Iliovasilema Grill € Quiet little taverna at the entrance of the village which overlooks countryside. Serves authentic Greek grills and tasty salads. ⓐ Keri village ☎ 26950 43270

Skaltsas Taverna € Situated on the junction leading to the beach at Keri Lake. Friendly service and picturesque countryside. ⓐ Keri Lake ☎ 26950 48798

Thraka €€ Home-reared grilled meats, traditional village bread, house wine, low prices and good service make this a pleasant stop on the way to see the sunset at Kampi or if you're visiting the Keri caves. ⓐ Macherado village ☎ 26950 92237

THE ISLAND OF PAXOS

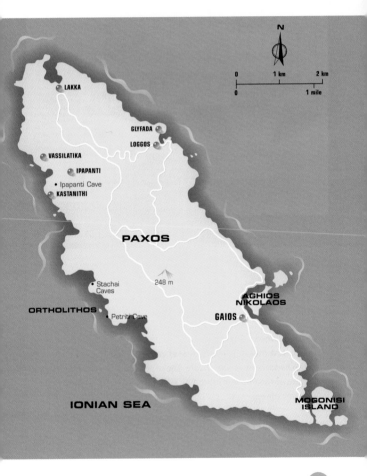

N

| 0 | 1 km | 2 km |
| 0 | | 1 mile |

LAKKA

GLYFADA

LOGGOS

VASSILATIKA

IPAPANTI

• Ipapanti Cave

KASTANITHI

PAXOS

248 m

• Stachai Caves

ORTHOLITHOS

• Petriti Cave

AGHIOS NIKOLAOS

GAIOS

IONIAN SEA

MOGONISI ISLAND

🔺 *Gaios harbour*

Gaios
a chic and cosmopolitan capital

**Gaios (pronounced 'Guy-yoss') bustles with visitors who fill the
waterside tavernas or pass the time of day watching elegant boats
from the handsome village square. The capital, with its winding streets
and whitewashed houses cascading with flowers, has a relaxed, easy-
going atmosphere.**

The town beach at Yiannos lies to the south of town and there's another
fine sandy beach and turquoise waters at Mogonissi islet, easily reached
by water-taxi from Gaios.

THINGS TO SEE & DO

Paxos Museum ★

This small museum, now housed in a former school building, contains a reconstruction of a Paxiot home, old national costumes and artefacts. ⓐ Waterfront ❶ 26620 32556 ⓛ Open summer only 19.30–20.30, closed Mon ❶ Admission charge

RESTAURANTS & BARS

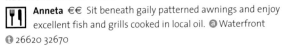

Anneta €€ Sit beneath gaily patterned awnings and enjoy excellent fish and grills cooked in local oil. ⓐ Waterfront ❶ 26620 32670

O Faros €€ Fish, grills and Greek specialities in comfortable outdoor taverna. Popular with holidaying Italians and yachties from Corfu. ⓐ Waterfront ❶ 26620 31345

Genesis Bar €€ Great cocktails and good music with views of the wooded islet of Aghios Nikolaos opposite and the statue of local 19th-century war hero, Yiorgos Anemogiannis. ⓐ Waterfront ❶ 26620 32495

George's Corner € Corner fast-food snack bar offering burgers and mezedes. Good streetside location in lively part of the town. ⓐ North side of the village square ❶ 26620 32362

Pan & Theo €€ Pastas, pizzas and fresh fish with waterside views. ⓐ Waterfront ❶ 26620 32458

Petrino €€ Fashionable music bar. ⓐ Next door to George's Corner ❶ 26620 32025

Volcano €€€ Fine wines, fine food and sophisticated atmosphere in this family-run taverna beside the church. ⓐ South side of the village square ❶ 26620 32251

Lakka
turquoise bays and verdant hills

Lakka (as in 'lacquer') lies on Paxos' northern tip and its picturesque harbour surrounded by verdant hills attracts yachting groups and people in search of peace and quiet. The island's oldest church stands nearby and from a ruined windmill you can see Corfu and Albania. Three small, pebbly beaches provide good snorkelling, water-skiing, windsurfing, sailing and scuba diving, or you can relax in a good choice of tavernas and bars. South of Lakka is the white-pebble beach of Malathendri where the fish are so friendly they literally eat out of your hand.

◆ *There are many ways to get out on the water*

THINGS TO SEE & DO

Aquarium Lakka ★★

Over 100 species of fish from local waters are displayed in 27 tanks. The display changes every year but expect to see moray and conger eel, octopus and lobster. ❷ On the Gaios road near the bus stop ❶ 26620 31389 ◷ Open 10.00–14.00 and 18.30–21.00 ❶ Admission charge

RESTAURANTS

Fanis €€ Comfortable seating in this waterfront café with views of fishing boats and friendly ducks. Ask for the Greek doughnuts, which come freshly cooked and oozing with honey. ❷ Waterfront ❶ 26620 31939

Klimataria € Famous for Eccles cakes baked by English proprietor. If you're missing home, try the cottage pie. Features outdoor seating under a grapevine in the smaller of the two village squares. ❶ 26620 30075

La Rosa di Paxos €€€ Up-market dining on flower-filled terrace on the waterfront; Italian specialities and fish. Fine selection of wines. ❷ Waterfront ❶ 26620 31471

To Steki €€ Friendly, family-run taverna serving grills, whitebait, fried squid or prawns. ❷ Waterfront ❶ 26620 31704

MUSIC FESTIVAL

During the first two weeks of September, Paxos plays host to the Paxos Chamber Music Festival when young artists from all over Europe arrive to perform at free concerts in Gaios. These concerts are very popular and are attended by famous musical personalities, who act as artistic directors. Look out for posters advertising the venues or see your rep.

Loggos
a tiny and intimate hide-away

This small resort has a pebbly beach to the north of the village. Even more laid back than Lakka, it sees fewer visitors but livens up during the holiday season. Small fishing boats bob in the harbour backed by wooded headlands of olive groves and pine trees which slope gently towards the white pebble beach of Levrechi just a five-minute walk from the centre.

RESTAURANTS

Evopi Snack Bar € Small and cosy with a special selection of coffees and delicious ice creams. Or try a cool beer and enjoy picturesque views of the harbour. ⓐ Waterfront ① 26620 31711

O Gios €€ Popular fish taverna – daily catch of octopus and squid. Fine selection of wines. Informal atmosphere. ⓐ Waterfront ① 26620 31735 ① Open for lunch and dinner

Gonia €€ With a cornerside location, this family-run taverna serves traditional Greek meals and is so photogenic that artists come to paint the scenic surroundings. ⓐ Waterfront ① 26620 31060

Nassos €€ Seafood is this taverna's speciality but grills are also served. For pleasant and panoramic views of the harbour, there's a separate upstairs terrace. ⓐ Waterfront ① 26620 31604

Taverna Vassilis €€ Close to the town beach, this family-run taverna has seating outside in a pretty flower-filled alleyway. ⓐ Waterfront ① 26620 31587

Yannis €€ Eat fresh fish in the courtyard of this taverna located in a quiet location at the back of the town. ⓐ 80 m (85 yds) from Loggos harbour, next to Sofia's Apartments ① 26620 31631

Paxos excursions
sea caves and olive groves

● *Rural life can be very different from the resorts*

Anti-Paxos ★★★

The beaches here are said to rival those of the Caribbean so unsurprisingly Anti-Paxos attracts hundreds of day-trippers. But to see Anti-Paxos at its very best, take an evening excursion from Gaios when the crowds have gone and enjoy a swim at Voutoumi Beach. A stop at the 7th-century church of Aghios Emelianos displays fine paintings and you can visit the small settlement of Vigla where vineyards and fruit orchards burst with pomegranates, figs and apricots. There is only one taverna at Voutoumi Beach and another high above the beach with exquisite views.

Northern villages ★

Paxos is a walker's paradise best explored by taking a guided walk following goat and mule tracks which wend their way past sleepy villages. On the way you can visit the island's only Byzantine church at Ipapanti, the stunning cliffs of Kastanida and stop for refreshments at a Venetian stone mansion at Vassilatika near Lakka.

Parga ★★★

Excursion boats leave for Parga (see page 32) on the Greek mainland where you can take in the ruins of Nekromanteion, discover the Oracle of the Dead and finish with a swim in the River Styx.

Sea caves ★★★

Paxos' west coast is rugged with high cliffs and magnificent sea caves which can only be discovered by boat. Many people take excursion boats from Gaios to visit the impressive 183 m (600 ft) high caves of Kastanithi, the monolith-fronted Ortholithos and the biggest cave called Grammatiko.

Athens
capital of ancient and modern Greece

With one foot in the ancient Greek past and the other firmly in the modern age, Athens is a fascinating city. World-famous sites such as the Parthenon, the Temple of Zeus and Hadrian's Arch have proved an irresistible attraction to travellers since the age of the Grand Tour. A visit to Athens, even if it means a 2-day excursion, is an experience that will live long in your memory.

Olympia

Some, though not all, excursions to Athens break the journey at Olympia, home of the ancient Olympic Games, which took place every four years from 776 BC to AD 393. Traditional hostilities between rival Greek states were halted temporarily for the duration of the Games, so that athletes from all over Greece could travel in safety to compete for the top honours. The site of the games lies below wooded Mount Kronos, and the excellent museum explains the development of the surviving temples and sports stadia. ☎ 26240 22517 ⏰ Open 08.00–19.00 (summer); 08.00–17.00 (winter) ❶ Admission charge

Athenian highlights

You could easily spend a day at the Acropolis, the massive hilltop sanctuary created under the rule of Pericles in the 5th century BC. Here the ancient Athenians built temples, theatres, exercise areas and colonnaded walkways to encourage high-minded citizens to worship Athena, Goddess of Wisdom, whose famous Parthenon temple crowns the site. All is explained in the excellent **Acropolis Museum** (☎ 21032 10219 ⏰ Open 08.00–19.00 in summer; 08.30–15.00 in winter ❶ Admission charge).

North of the Acropolis is the chic Kolonaki district, where you will find a whole clutch of world-class museums. If you only have time to do one, make it the **National Archaeological Museum** (☎ 44 Patission ☎ 21082 17717 ⏰ Open Mon 12.30–18.45, Tues–Fri 08.00–18.45, Sat and Sun 08.30–14.45 ❶ Admission charge), whose exhibits include the golden

● *The Acropolis is world-famous for its ancient ruins, most notably the Parthenon*

mask of Agamemnon, and the boldly abstract Cycladic sculptures dating back to the 3rd millennium BC.

On the way to the museum you may well get lost in the warren of alleys packed with shops and craft workshops in the **Plaka** district below the Parthenon (also known, confusingly, as the Monastiraki area and the Flea Market). Shop here for all sorts of bargains, including leather sandals and bags, modern icons painted using ancient techniques, gold and silver jewellery, clothing and all sorts of traditional crafts.

A good place to rendezvous is **Syntagma Square**, with its Parliament Building, where you can watch the Changing of the Evzone Guard, on the hour every hour. On Sundays and special occasions these crack troops wear a special white pleated kilt, in memory of the costumes worn by freedom fighters during the Greek War of Independence (1821–31).

 The best views over Athens are from Lykavitos Hill. It is a strenuous walk to the top but a funicular railway operates every 30 minutes from the corner of Ploutarchou Street, just north of Kolonaki Square (buy a return ticket). The views are unforgettable and there is a very expensive restaurant at the top.

RESTAURANTS

Daphne €€€ For an unusual dining experience, dress up for this up-market restaurant complete with Pompeiian frescos. Huge menu of traditional Greek and international fare. Book ahead. ⓐ 4 Lisikratous Street, Plaka ⓣ 21032 27971

Platanos €€ Order traditional Greek food in one of the oldest restaurants in the Plaka district and relax beneath the shade of a massive plane tree. ⓐ 4 Diogenis Street, Plaka ⓣ 21032 20666 ⓛ Closed Mon

Thanasis € The best place in town for souvlaki (kebabs with pitta bread and salad). Plenty of outdoor seating. ⓐ Mitropoleos 69, Monastiraki ⓣ 21032 44705

Food & drink

THE GREEK TAVERNA

The Greek taverna is a wonderfully flexible institution. You are made equally welcome, whether you just want to settle down with a beer and a plate of chips or Greek salad, or whether you arrive with a group of friends to sample a mezedes feast, enjoying the seemingly endless variety and succession of little dishes that emerge from the kitchen.

Some tavernas have an extensive menu featuring everything from simple grilled chicken to fresh fish sold by the weight. Others have no formal menu: the waiter will tell you what is available or, better still, you

will be invited into the kitchen to view the range of prepared dishes and daily specials on offer. You place your order by pointing to the dishes you want. If you do order prepared food, do not be disappointed if the moussaka or stuffed tomatoes are served lukewarm – this is the traditional Greek way, and the food will usually be reheated if you ask.

STARTERS

Many Greek starters are now familiar to everyone through the products sold on supermarket shelves throughout Europe, but every taverna has its own recipe or its own style of

● Stuffed vine leaves

presenting such typical dishes as taramasalata (smoked cod's roe beaten with potatoes, lemon juice and oil) and tzatziki (yoghurt dip with cucumber and garlic).

More unusual dishes to look out for are *gigantes* (fresh butter beans cooked in tomato sauce), *melitzanasalata* (aubergine dip, sometimes served with tomatoes), *arakas* (peas in herb dressing), *dolmades* (vine leaves stuffed with herb-flavoured rice) or *saganaki* (grilled or fried cheese). Typically, a Greek salad *(horiatiki salata)* will consist of lettuce, onion, cucumber, tomatoes and olives with a chunk of feta (crumbly white sheep's milk cheese) on top – almost a meal in itself.

◀ A typical Greek dish

MAIN COURSES

Taverna staples include *moussaka* (minced lamb layered with potatoes, aubergines and white sauce) and *kleftiko* (lamb with herbs, baked in foil in the oven until it is meltingly tender). Minced beef, lamb, pork or veal can be used to make spicy meatballs called *soutsoukakia* (sausage-shaped) and *keftedes* (round), often served in tomato sauce. *Pastitsio* (sometimes called *pasticio*) is a delicious layered pie made from minced meat, macaroni, tomatoes, cheese and white sauce, reflecting Venetian influence on Greek cuisine.

Stifado is the term for any casserole; though usually made from veal, each island has its own variations on this Greek staple, made from rabbit or tender chunks of beef, cooked long and slow with herbs, vinegar, tomatoes, onions and garlic. Grilling over a wood or charcoal fire adds a special flavour to chicken, *souvlakia* (skewered cubes of pork or veal, flavoured with oregano), *kalamari* (squid) or *barbounia* (red mullet). As a concession to visitors, some tavernas serve doner kebab, though this spit roast meat, served in pitta-bread pockets with salad and sauce, is traditionally sold from specialist fast-food stalls rather than restaurants.

Fresh fish can be the most expensive dish on the menu, but the price is worth paying for a special night out – most restaurant menus will state whether the fish is fresh or frozen, and the price should reflect this, with frozen *garides* (prawns), for example, being a third of the price of fresh ones. If you like fish but do not want to spend a fortune, go for *marides* – whitebait – for a delicious and inexpensive meal.

GREEK TAKE-AWAY

Greek fast food is designed to fill that hole that develops mid-morning or at any time of day when you are on the move. Bakers and kiosks sell little pies made from filo pastry and deliciously filled with cheese *(tiropitta)*, spinach *(spanakopitta)* or minced lamb *(kreatopitta)*. For sweet-lovers, there is *bougatza*, bursting with delicious vanilla custard, or apple-filled *milopitta*.

VEGETARIANS

Greek restaurants make good use of seasonal fruit and vegetables, and if you get to know the taverna owner, they may well prepare something just for you, given a day's notice – meat-free stuffed tomatoes or peppers, for example. Among dishes found in many tavernas, look for *briam* (similar to ratatouille, and made from aubergines, peppers, courgettes and tomatoes), *melitzanes fournou* (baked aubergines – usually made with onions and tomatoes), *fassolia* and *bamyes* (green beans and okra, respectively, cooked in a herb-rich tomato sauce) and *kolokithea tiganita* (courgettes fried in batter).

DESSERTS

Greeks go to a *kafeneion* (café) or *zacharoplasteio* (pastry shop) if they want sweet desserts, though tavernas have adapted to visitors to the degree that they may well offer fresh fruit, fruit salad, ice cream or a velvety smooth dish of yoghurt and honey. At a café, the choice of pastries is much wider: look for *baklava* (filo pastry, honey and nuts), *kadaifi* (shredded wheat and nuts drenched with honey syrup) and *loukoumades* (honey and cinnamon-flavoured doughnuts). You will also find nougat and *halva* (a dessert made from sesame paste, honey and nuts) on offer.

DRINKS

Retsina is the best-known Greek wine, and you will find it on the wine list everywhere you go in Greece. Flavoured with pine resin, it is a taste that, once acquired, can become addictive. If you prefer something truly local, ask for house wine, which will be served to you in a jug, often drawn direct from a large barrel. These wines are so cheap that you can experiment, and most of the time they will be pleasant and refreshing. Two other drinks are commonly served in Greek cafés. *Ouzo* has a strong aniseed taste, which you will either love or hate – try it with ice and water, or with lemonade or fresh orange juice. *Metaxa* is Greek brandy, and the higher the number of stars (3, 5 or 7) the better the quality. You could also ask for the drier *kamba*.

Menu decoder

Here are some of the authentic Greek dishes that you might encounter in tavernas or pastry shops.

dolmadákia Vine leaves stuffed with rice, onions and currants, dill, parsley, mint and lemon juice

domátes/piperiés yemistés Tomatoes/peppers stuffed with herb-flavoured rice (and sometimes minced lamb or beef)

fassólia saláta White beans (haricot, butter beans) dressed with olive oil, lemon juice, parsley, onions, olives and tomato

lazánia sto fourno Greek lasagne, similar to Italian lasagne, but often including additional ingredients, such as chopped boiled egg or sliced Greek-style sausages

makaronópita A pie made from macaroni blended with beaten eggs, cheese and milk, baked in puff pastry

melitzanópita Pie made from baked liquidised aubergines mixed with onions, garlic, breadcrumbs, eggs, mint and parmesan cheese

melitzanosaláta Aubergine dip made from baked aubergines, liquidized with tomatoes, onions and lemon juice

mezedes A selection of appetisers, such as *tzatziki*, *dolmadákia* and *melitzano saláta*

THE KAFENEION

In Greek villages, the *kafeneion* (café) remains very much a male preserve, although visitors of both sexes will be made welcome. Customers come here to read the paper, debate the issues of the day and play backgammon, as well as to consume *elinikos kafés* (Greek coffee). This is made by boiling finely ground beans in a special pot with a long handle. Sugar is added during the preparation rather than at the table, so you should order *glyko* (sweet), *metrio* (medium) or *sketo* (no sugar). In summer, try *frappé* (with ice).

moussakás Moussaka, made from fried slices of aubergines, interlayered with minced beef and béchemel sauce

pastítsio Layers of macaroni, parmesan cheese and minced meat (cooked with onions, tomatoes and basil), topped with *béchemel* sauce and baked

píta me kymá Meat pie made from minced lamb and eggs, flavoured with onions and cinnamon and baked in filo pastry

saláta Aubergine dip made from baked aubergines, liquidised with tomatoes, onions and lemon juice

saláta horiátiki Country salad (known in England as 'Greek salad'); every restaurant has its own recipe, but the basic ingredients are tomatoes, cucumber, onions, green peppers, black olives, oregano and feta cheese dressed with vinegar, olive oil and oregano

souvláki Kebab usually of pork cooked over charcoal

spanakotyropitákia Cigar-shaped pies made from feta cheese, eggs, spinach, onions and nutmeg in filo pastry

taramosaláta Cod's roe dip made from pureed potatoes, smoked cod's roe, oil, lemon juice and onion

tyropitákia small triangular cheese pies made from feta cheese and eggs in filo pastry

tzatzíki Grated cucumber and garlic in a dressing of yoghurt, olive oil and vinegar

▶ *Experiment with local wines*

Shopping

Tourist shops in the Ionian Islands open all hours, including Sundays, and they accept credit cards for all but the smallest of purchases. Local shops have more restricted hours and are usually closed over lunch, and all day Sunday. You may want to shop in local shops and markets for some typically Greek souvenirs, such as worry beads, or – if you have fallen in love with the lively tones of bouzouki music – some music cassettes featuring your favourite Greek melodies. Other typically local goods include honey, nougat, dried herbs, cheeses, olives and decorative ceramic pots.

DESIGNER GOODS & PERFUMES

Calvin Klein sweatshirts, Levi jeans, Joop handbags, Lacoste and Ralph Lauren polo shirts, Rolex watches, Christian Dior perfumes and dozens of other top name products can be bought in souvenir shops at a fraction of their usual price – this is because they are fakes. If this does not deter you, examine the goods very carefully for quality of workmanship (check for loose stitching, etc) before you part with your money. There are some bargains to be had.

JEWELLERY

Greece produces many excellent designs in gold and silver, and the prices for handmade earrings, rings, bracelets, medallions and necklaces are very competitive with the cost of mass-produced jewellery sold back home. Gold is graded in carats, from 14 (the cheapest) up to 24, and silver is graded according to its purity, 1000 being pure silver. Designs range from the ultra modern to copies of ancient Greek jewellery.

LEATHER

Another Greek speciality, leather goods are of exceptional quality and workmanship, and competitively priced. Treat yourself to a purse, wallet or handbag, or buy school satchels for the children or some sandals for the beach.

🔺 *Markets are a source of both souvenirs and useful items*

RUGS & TEXTILES

So many hours of hard work go into the production of hand-woven carpets and embroidered table-cloths or cushion covers that you would not expect them to be cheap. Even so, if you see something you really like, buy it – because it will be considerably cheaper here, bought direct from the producer, than from a shop or department store back home.

⬤ *There's lots to keep children amused on the islands*

Kids

BOAT TRIPS

Young children love boat trips. Interesting excursions are available from
Nidri (see page 22) and Vassiliki (see page 25), or from Zante to the
Kianou Caves (see page 82). Better still, get together with some other
parents and charter a boat – if there are a number of you it will not cost
a lot. You can decide with the owner where to go – seek out some small
private cove and play at being stranded on a desert island for the day.

EATING OUT

Greeks love children and Greek families all eat out together, so your children will be more than welcome in the local taverna, where they will probably make friends very quickly with the other children, despite the language barrier. Most restaurants catering for tourists have a special children's menu featuring such favourites as chicken, pizza, beefburgers or fish fingers, and quite a number have a play area. Children in Greece stay up late at night, catching up on lost sleep during the afternoon siesta – a habit you might want to emulate to avoid the intense heat of the Greek midday.

EXCURSIONS

Given a basic interest in history and a little bit of briefing by mum and dad, a half-day spent scampering around the ruins of Nekromanteion (see page 37) or an ancient city like Olympia (see page 92), on the Greek mainland, can be a real success.

SPORTS & PASTIMES

Facilities vary greatly from resort to resort (check pages 13–94 for resort-specific details). Horse riding is available at Vassiliki (see page 25) and Kalamaki (see page 70), and you may find there is a smaller stable near to you. There are go-karting clubs on several of the islands. On Zante, try Laganas Go-Kart & Crazy Golf (see page 66) or Mini Golf in Kalamaki (see page 70). Ask your tour rep, hotel or the tourist office for further information about activities in your area.

WATER SPORTS

Older children who are confident swimmers will love the range of water sports on offer at many beaches. Vassiliki is famous for windsurfing (see page 24), but it's also available at Valtos (see page 34) and Tsivili (see page 79). For excellent snorkelling, try Agiofili (see page 25) or Skala (see page 54). For the not so brave, several beaches also have pedalos for hire, which offer an opportunity to explore the clear inshore waters, looking for fish and spotting loggerhead turtles.

Sports & activities

ENJOY YOURSELF ON LAND & SEA

The island resorts are all well supplied with facilities for sports, including tennis and mini-golf. You can also choose from a growing range of water sports that will test your skill and sense of adventure (be sure to check first, however, whether your insurance policy covers you).

Your best bet, if you want to try out windsurfing, sailing, paragliding, water-skiing or scuba diving, is to sign up for a training course with one of the water sports centres that are based in the main resorts. Top instructors will adapt their instruction to your level of competence, so even intermediate and advanced level tuition is available.

If the idea of water sports fills you with horror for whatever reason, seek out a beach where motorised sports are banned. There are many quiet coves where peace and quiet reign, and on Zante most water sports are banned in the Laganas Bay area to protect the Loggerhead Turtles.

BELOW THE WATER

Warm, crystal-clear waters make the Ionian Islands a wonderful place to go diving. There are several schools where equipment can be hired and where a range of courses is available at every level, from beginners to experienced divers. Always look for the initials PADI (Professional Association of Diving Instructors) or BSAC (British Sub-Aqua Club) as a mark that the school conforms to the highest professional standards.

WALKING & CYCLING

Walking and cycling allow you to adjust to the pace of the real Greece, explore sleepy villages and archaeological sites, observe nature at close quarters, and understand better the agricultural way of life in Greece. You can hire mountain bikes in many resorts, and trail maps and information leaflets are available from some tourist offices in the island capitals. Two of the best areas for getting out and about are the mountains of Lefkas, with their breathtaking scenery, and the east coast of Zante which, being flat, is popular with cyclists and easy to explore.

● *Sign up for a windsurfing course.*

SUMMER FLOWERS

The Ionian Islands are renowned for their wild flowers, but you have to come in spring (March to June) for the best displays. In summer, you will see the hardy sea daffodil, with its sweetly scented white flower, which uses its huge bulb as a reservoir of food and water during the hottest months. Other plants flowering at this time of year are bougainvillaea, with its thorny stems and purple flowers, pink-flowered oleanders and rock roses.

Festivals & events

There are two ways to get under the skin of Greek culture, both of them equally enjoyable. One is to attend a Greek evening and the other is to take part in a festival. Folk evenings can be artificial events put on for tourists, but on the Ionian Islands the music and dance you will experience during a typical Greek evening is part of a living culture. Kantathes (folk songs) still play a vital part in village festivals, and they can be heard all over the islands in tavernas where local people sing to entertain each other. Equally popular is the haunting mandolin-like melody of the bouzouki.

Festivals are common in the summer months when local people celebrate the name day of the patron saint of their church or monastery. These festivals, called *panayiria*, are religious in focus, but eating, drinking, music and dancing play a central role. Street vendors set up stalls selling local products and there is usually a barbecue selling delicious grilled foods.

EASTER

Zante is one of the most festive of the islands, with a two-week carnival leading up to Shrove Tuesday, followed a few weeks later by the Holy Week celebrations. Greek Orthodox Easter can be anything from one to three weeks later than Easter in the western calendar and so may coincide with your visit. This colourful celebration begins at midnight on Easter Saturday, when rifle shots are heard and fireworks light up the sky to welcome the news that Christ is risen. On the Sunday, lamb is roasted over great open-air barbecues, and eaten for lunch, with sweet cinnamon-flavoured Easter biscuits to follow, all washed down by bottles of wine from the previous autumn's vintage.

Fireworks are a feature of Easter celebrations on Zante

⬢ *Traditional dancing*

AGHIOS DIONYSIOS

The feast of Aghios Dionysios – better known as St Dennis, the patron saint of Zante – is celebrated on 24 August. It is believed that St Dennis still walks the island and that his slippers wear out (see page 59), so they are replaced annually when the silver casket that holds his mummified remains is opened on 24 August. St Dennis's body is then paraded around the town centre and harbour area. In the evening a carnival atmosphere takes over the island. Market stalls are erected throughout Zante Town and a procession is held to the sound of local bands and exploding fireworks.

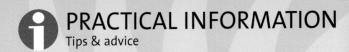

Preparing to go

GETTING THERE

The cheapest way to get to the Ionian Islands is to book a package holiday with one of the leading tour operators specialising in Ionian Islands holidays. You should also check the Travel supplements of the weekend newspapers, such as the *Sunday Telegraph*, and *The Sunday Times*. They often carry adverts for inexpensive flights, as well as classified adverts for privately owned villas and apartments to rent in most popular holiday destinations. If your travelling times are flexible, and if you can avoid the school holidays, you can also find some very cheap last-minute deals using the websites for the leading holiday companies.

BEFORE YOU LEAVE

It is not necessary to have inoculations to travel in Europe, but you should make sure you and your family are up to date with the basics, such as tetanus. It is a good idea to pack a small first-aid kit to carry with you containing plasters, antiseptic cream, travel sickness pills, insect repellent and/or bite relief cream, antihistamine tablets, upset stomach remedies and painkillers. Sun lotion can be more expensive in the Ionian Islands than in the UK so it is worth taking a good selection, especially of the higher-factor lotions if you have children with you, and don't forget after-sun cream as well. If you are taking prescription medicines, ensure that you take enough for the duration of your visit – you may find it impossible to obtain the same medicines in the Ionian Islands. It is also worth having a dental check-up before you leave.

DOCUMENTS

The most important documents you will need are your tickets and your passport. Check well in advance that your passport is up to date and has at least three months left to run (six months is even better). All children, including newborn babies, need their own passport now, unless they are already included on the passport of the person they are travelling with. It generally takes at least three weeks to process a passport renewal. This can be longer in the run-up to the summer months. Contact the **Passport Agency** for the latest information on how to renew your passport and the processing times involved. ☎ 0870 521 0410 Ⓦ www.ukpa.gov.uk

You should check the details of your travel tickets well before your departure, ensuring that the timings and dates are correct.

If you are thinking of hiring a car while you are away, you will need to have your UK driving licence with you. If you want more than one driver for the car, the other drivers must have their licences too.

MONEY

You will need some currency before you go, especially if your flight gets you to your destination at the weekend or late in the day after the banks have closed. Traveller's cheques are the safest way to carry money because the money will be refunded if the cheques are lost or stolen. To buy traveller's cheques or exchange money at a bank you may need to give up to a week's notice, depending on the quantity of foreign currency you require. You can exchange money at the airport before you depart. You should also make sure that your credit and debit cards are up to date – you do not want them to expire mid holiday – and that your credit limit is sufficient to allow you to make those holiday purchases. Don't forget, too, to check your PIN numbers in case you haven't used them for a while – you may want to draw money from cash dispensers while you are away. Ring your bank or card company and they will help you out.

INSURANCE

Have you got sufficient cover for your holiday? Check that your policy covers you adequately for loss of possessions and valuables, for activities you might want to try – such as scuba-diving, horse-riding, or water sports – and for emergency medical and dental treatment, including flights home if required.

It is essential to take an E111 form (available from post offices) to take with you, to ensure that if you have any medical treatment while away you can reclaim the costs incurred on your return. After January 2006, a new EHIC card replaces the E111 form to allow UK-visitors access to reduced-cost and somethimes free state-provided medical treatment in the EEA. For further information, ring EHIC enquiries line: ☎ 0845 605 0707 or visit the Department of Health website: 🌐 www.dh.gov.uk

CLIMATE

The weather you're likely to find depends on when you visit. July and August are the hottest months, with maximum daytime temperatures going over 40°C (104°F). June and September are slightly cooler, with daytime temperatures rarely exceeding 30°C (86°F). During late-May and early-October, it's still just about possible to swim, but the weather can be unpredictable, with temperatures rarely exceeding 25°C (77°F). In high season, pack some light cotton clothes so you can cover up when you've had enough sun. Even during summer, temperatures can drop dramatically at night, so you should also bring at least one light jumper or jacket.

TELEPHONING GREECE
To call Greece from the UK, dial 00 30 followed by the 10-digit number in full.

SECURITY

Take sensible precautions to prevent your house being burgled:

- Cancel milk, newspapers and other regular deliveries so that post and milk does not pile up on the doorstep, indicating that you are away.
- Let the postman know where to leave parcels and bulky mail that will not go through your letterbox – ideally with a next-door neighbour.
- If possible, arrange for a friend or neighbour to visit regularly or consider buying electrical devices that will switch lights and radios on and off, again to give the impression that there is someone in.
- Let Neighbourhood Watch representatives know that you will be away so that they can keep an eye on your home.
- If you have a burglar alarm, make sure that it is serviced and working

properly and is switched on when you leave (you may find that your insurance policy requires this). Ensure that a neighbour is able to gain access to the alarm to turn it off if it is set off accidentally.

- If you are leaving cars unattended, put them in a garage, if possible, and leave a key with a neighbour in case the alarm goes off.

AIRPORT PARKING & ACCOMMODATION

If you intend to leave your car in an airport car park while you are away, or stay the night at an airport hotel before or after your flight, you should book well ahead to take advantage of discounts or cheap off-airport parking. Airport accommodation gets booked up several weeks in advance, especially during the height of the holiday season. Check whether the hotel offers free parking for the duration of the holiday.

BAGGAGE ALLOWANCE

Baggage allowances vary according to the airline, destination and the class of travel, but 20kg (44lb) per person is the norm for luggage that is carried in the hold (it usually tells you what the weight limit is on your ticket). You are also allowed one item of cabin baggage weighing no more than 5kg (11lb), and measuring 46 by 30 by 23cm (18 by 12 by 9 inches). In addition, you can usually carry your duty-free purchases, umbrella, handbag, coat, etc, as hand baggage. Large items – golf-clubs, collapsible wheelchairs, etc – are usually charged as extras. It is a good idea to let the airline know in advance that you want to bring these.

CHECK-IN, PASSPORT CONTROL & CUSTOMS

First-time travellers can often find airports stressful, but it is all very easy.

- Check-in desks usually open two or three hours before the flight is due to depart. Arrive early for the best choice of seats.
- Look for your flight number on the TV monitors in the check-in area, and find your check-in desk. Take your boarding card to the departure gate where your hand luggage is X-rayed and your passport checked.
- You can shop and relax in the departure area, but watch the monitors that tell you when to board – usually about 30 minutes before take-off.

During your stay

AIRPORTS

There are direct flights from various airports in the UK to the islands of Kefalonia and Zante. Both these islands are also served by daily flights (Olympic Airways Ⓦ www.olympic-airways.gr) from Athens, and linked to one another by twice-weekly flights through summer. Kefalonia airport (❶ 26710 41511) lies 8 km (5 miles) south of Argostoli, while Zante airport (❶ 26950 28322) is a short distance southwest of Zante Town. There are no airport buses, so you'll need to take a taxi to your hotel.

BEACHES

In summer, many beaches have life guards and a flag safety system. Make sure that you are familiar with the flag system for the Ionian Islands. Other beaches may also be safe for swimming but there are unlikely to be any lifeguards or life-saving amenities available. Bear in mind that the strong winds that can develop in the hotter summer months can quickly change a safe beach into a not-so-safe one, and on some beaches the current in the sea gets stronger the further out that you go. If in doubt, ask your local representative or at your hotel.

CHILDREN'S ACTIVITIES

Children love the seaside and you'll find plenty of beaches with shallow water safe for paddling. Depending on where you stay, there may also be facilities for go-karting and horse riding. Family life is important in Greece, and children are very welcome in restaurants and cafés, even late at night.

CONSULATES

There is a British Vice Consulate in **Zante Town** (ⓐ 5 Foskolo ❶ 26950 22906). If you are staying on Lefkas, Paxos or in Parga, you may find it more convenient to contact the British Consulate on **Corfu** (ⓐ 2 Alexandras ❶ 26610 30055), or if you are on Kefalonia there is one in **Patras** (ⓐ Votsi 2 ❶ 2610 277329). The **British Embassy** is in Athens (ⓐ 1 Ploutarhou ❶ 210 7272600 Ⓦ www.british-embassy.gr).

CURRENCY

Currency along with 11 other EU countries, Greece adopted the euro (€) in 2002. Greeks complain that the cost of living has consequently risen, and you may well notice a slight increase in prices if you've been here before. Euro note denominations are 5, 10, 20, 50, 100 and 200. Coins are 1, 2, 5, 10, 20 and 50 cents/lepta, and 1 and 2 €.

Banks Expect queues at banks. 🕒 Open Mon to Thurs 08.00–14.00, Fri 08.00–13.30. Branches in tourist centres may open later and on Sat. Take your passport when changing money or traveller's cheques.

Credit cards Essential for care hire. If paying by card, have your passport with you, and check first that card payment is accepted, particularly away from resorts and town.

ELECTRICITY

Like the rest of mainland Europe, Greece uses double round-pin plugs (220 volt AC). So if you plan to bring any electrical equipment, make sure you buy an adaptor in the UK before you set off, as they are difficult to find on the islands. If you are considering buying electrical appliances to take home, always check that they will work in the UK before you buy.

FACILITIES FOR THE DISABLED

Facilities on the islands are not very well developed for the disabled, though Greeks are generally courteous and ready to help anyone with difficulties. Most modern hotels have lifts, but you should ask about other facilities before booking.

BEACH SAFETY

A flag system is used to warn bathers when sea conditions are unsafe for swimming.

- **Red flag** = dangerous conditions, no swimming
- **Yellow** = good swimmers only, apply caution
- **Green** = safe bathing conditions

GETTING AROUND

Car hire and driving If you're over 21 (25 in some cases) and have a British driving licence, you can hire a car in any of the main towns, or from Kefalonia and Zante airports. Greeks drive on the right. The maximum speed limit is 110 km/h (60 mph) on main roads and 50 km/h (31 mph) in built-up areas. Seat belts must be worn and children aged under 10 must sit in the back seat. Penalties for drinking and driving over the limit are severe. If you intend to hire a **moped** or **motorbike**, check that your travel insurance policy covers you (many policies specifically exclude this). Always wear a crash helmet (the law requires this) and drive safely.

Breaking down The Greek Automobile and Touring Club (ELPA) provide 24-hr breakdown assistance (📞 104). This is expensive, but free if you can prove you're a member of the AA or RAC.

Public transport Public transport is cheap and efficient by British standards. While on the islands, you can reach almost any neighbouring town, village and even most beaches by local bus. From Parga you can take a bus inland to Ioannina, Zagoria and the monasteries of the Meteora. See 🌐 www.ktel.org for bus timetables throughout Greece, including sections on Kefalonia and Lefkada, in English.

Ferries and boats During your stay on the islands, you can reach the mainland and most other neighbouring islands by boat: Lefkas is joined to the mainland by a bridge, but there are ferry services from Nidri and Vassiliki to Fiskardo (on Kefalonia).

Kefalonia has regular mainland connections from Sami to Patras, and Argostoli and Poros to Kylini, as well as services from Fiskardo to Nidri and Vassiliki (on the island of Lefkas), and from Pessada to Skinari(on Zante). On Kefalonia itself, the towns of Argostoli and Lixouri are also connected by boat.

Zante has a regular mainland connection from Zante Town to Kylini, as well as a service from Skinari to Pessada (Kefalonia). Paxos has a regular mainland connection from Gaios to Igoumenitsa, and in summer there's a service to Parga. It's also possible to take a hydrofoil from Gaios to the island of Corfu.

Taxis Taxis are cheap, especially if you club together and share the fare between three or four passengers. However, Greek taxi drivers have unfortunately earned themselves a reputation for ripping off foreigners. Journeys are priced by time and distance, and drivers are obliged by law to run a meter. There are surcharges for luggage and for trips to and from airports and ports.

HEALTH MATTERS

Chemists Most minor health problems can be solved by a visit to a chemist *(farmakio)*, easily found by the illuminated red or green cross displayed outside. Local chemists are highly trained and can supply certain medicines that are only available on doctor's prescription in the UK. Most speak good English. If closed, a sign on the door will tell you where the nearest open pharmacy is located. For more serious problems, go to the nearest hospital *(nosokomio)*, and if you have problems with your teeth, visit a dentist *(othondiatrio)*.

Health hazards Mosquitoes and sand-flies are the main biting hazards: insect repellents are available from most general stores, and pharmacies will sell cream to relieve the itch. When bathing, watch out for jellyfish, whose sting can result in a painful nettle-like rash; pharmacies sell remedies to lessen the sting, which will go down after a few hours. Wear something on your feet when exploring rocks to avoid sea urchins: soften the skin well with olive all and remove their spines with a needle, as you would a splinter.

Sunburn and sunstroke are also common problems, but can easily be avoided. Don't spend too long in the sun, wear a hat and drink plenty of water. Now that everyone is worried about the potentially harmful effects of the sun, even olive-skinned Greeks have started using protective creams, and you'll find a wide choice readily available in local stores.

Water Tap water is good for drinking throughout the country. However, due to possible high mineral contents, it is advisable to buy bottled mineral water for general daily use.

THE LANGUAGE

A difficult language, the beauty of Greek is that it is phonetic. Greeks love to hear visitors attempt to speak it. However, most signs are in Greek and English, and English is so widely – and well – spoken that you can happily trundle through a fortnight without needing a word of Greek.

The Greek alphabet

Greek	Name	Pronunciation	Greek	Name	Pronunciation
Α α	alpha	a (as in apple)	Ν ν	ni	n as in no
Β β	beta	v (as in vase)	Ξ ξ	xi	x/ks as in xerox
Γ γ	gamma	g/y, becomes y in front of e and i	Ο ο	omicron	o as in opera
			Π π	pi	p as in pope
Δ δ	delta	th as in the	Ρ ρ	rho	r as in roll
Ε ε	epsilon	e as in extra	Σ σ	sigma	s as in safe
Ζ ζ	zeta	z as in zest	Τ τ	taf	t as in table
Η η	eta	i/e as in eat	Υ υ	ypsilon	e as in these
Θ θ	theta	th as in theme	Φ φ	fi	f as in fire
Ι ι	iota	i/e as in these	Χ χ	hi	kh as in Bach
Κ κ	kappa	k/c as in keep	Ψ ψ	psi	ps as in corpse
Λ λ	lamda	l as in limit	Ω ω	omega	o as in opera
Μ μ	mi	m as in mother			

ENGLISH	GREEK (pronunciation)
General vocabulary	
yes/no	*neh/Okhee*
please/thank you	*parakahLO/efkhareesTO*
hello/goodbye	*YAsoo/andEEo*
good morning/good afternoon/evening	*kahleeMEHRa/kahleeSPEHRa*
good night	*kahleeNEEKHtah*
OK	*enDACKsee*
excuse me/sorry	*signomee*
Help!	*VoyIthia!*
today/tomorrow	*siMEHRa/AHvrio*
yesterday	*ektes*

ENGLISH	GREEK (pronunciation)
Useful words and phrases	
open/closed	*anikTON/klisTON*
right/left	*thexia/aristerA*
How much is it?	*POso kAni?*
Where is a bank/post office?	Poo Ine i TRApeza?/to tahithromEEo?
Where is the bus station?	*Poo Ine o stathMOS ton iperastiKON*
	leoforEEon?
stamp	*grammatOseemo*
doctor/hospital	*YAHtros/nosokoMEEo*
police	*assteenoMEEa*
I would like...	*Tha Ithela*
menu	*menOO*
toilets	*tooahLEHtess*
mineral water	*emfialoMENo nerO*
bread	*psomEE*
salt/pepper	*alAHti/pipEri*
fish/meat	*psarEE/krEas*
beer/wine	*bEEra/krasEE*
Cheers!	*Steen eeyEEa soo!/YAHmas!*
coffee with milk	*kafEs (me gAla)*
Can we have the bill, please?	*Mas fErnete ton logariasmO, parakalO?*
I don't understand/	*then katalaveno/MilAte*
Do you speak English?	*AnglikA?*

MEDIA

Newspapers In resort areas, a good selection of English newspapers is readily available at street kiosks. They tend to reach the islands the day after publishing.

Television On Greek TV, many English and American films are shown in original version with Greek sub-titles. Most good hotels have satellite TV, and some bars have big screens showing international sporting events.

OPENING HOURS

Opening hours vary greatly from town to town, store to store, though during summer almost everything shuts for afternoon siesta. The following hours are intended as a rough guideline, but are by no means foolproof:

Banks 🕐 Open Mon–Fri (some also Sat) 08.00–14.00.

Shops 🕐 Open Mon, Wed, Fri 09.00–14.00, and Tues, Thur 09.00–14.00 and 17.00–20.30. Tourist shops may stay open all day, seven days a week.

Churches The more important churches are open daily (🕐 08.00–19.00). Some smaller churches are kept locked, and opened only for appropriate Saints' days.

Pharmacies 🕐 Open Mon–Fri 09.00–14.00, with one open daily 24-hours in the larger towns.

Restaurants 🕐 Open for lunch 12.30–15.30, dinner 19.00–24.00, but some stay open all day.

Museums 🕐 Open Tues–Sat 09.00–14.00.

Public holidays 1 Jan (New Year's Day), 6 Jan (Epiphany), Lent Monday (date varies), 25 Mar (Independence Day), Easter Sunday (date varies), 1 May (Labour Day), Whit Monday, 15 Aug (Assumption), 28 Oct (Ohi Day), 25 and 26 Dec (Christmas).

PERSONAL COMFORT & SECURITY

Making a complaint Each resort town has its own Tourist Police (an off-shoot of the regular police), where you can lodge complaints against unsatisfactory hotels and restaurants.

Laundry and dry cleaning In the larger resort towns you'll find a laundry (*katharistirio*) and dry cleaners (*stegnokatharistiro*).

Public toilets Public toilets are found in bus stations and main squares. Smarter facilities are found in bars, but you should buy a drink if you are using them. Toilets are generally very clean, but there is one oddity throughout Greece: You can't flush away used toilet paper, but should put it in a bin (provided in each cubicle) next to the toilet. Remember this, or you risk blocking the pipes!

Lost property If you lose something valuable, report it immediately to the police and obtain a copy of your statement to support your insurance claim. Note – lost property reports to the police should be made at the location you lost the item(s) or police may refuse to make a report.

Valuables Take sensible precautions, and do not leave valuables unattended in a car or on the beach.

Crime Greece has one of lowest crime rates in Europe and is relatively safe by British standards. In fact, most crimes are committed by tourists! If you get into trouble, you have the right to contact the British Consulate, who will arrange a lawyer for you.

POST OFFICES

In most resort towns, the post office *(tahithromio)* works Mon-Fri 07.30-14.00. However, if you buy a postcard *(karta-postal)* from a street kiosk, you can also ask for a stamp *(gramatosimo)* there and then. Letterboxes are bright yellow.

RELIGION

Greeks are Orthodox Christians. The older people take religion very seriously, so remember to show respect when visiting churches. The most important religious celebration is the Orthodox Easter rather than Christmas (celebrated on 25 December).

EMERGENCY NUMBERS

For help in an emergency dial **100** for the police, **171** for the tourist police and **166** for an ambulance.

TELEPHONING ABROAD

To call an overseas number, dial oo (the international access code), then the country code (UK=44), then the area code minus the initial zero, followed by the number.

TELEPHONES

You can make calls from most newspaper kiosks – the call is metered and you pay when you have finished. Blue public call boxes are cheaper for overseas calls; to use one you'll need an OTE telephone card *(tilekarta)*, which can be bought at most newspaper kiosks and newsagents. For international telephone information dial ❶ 162. For local telephone information dial ❶ 131.

TIME DIFFERENCES

Greek time is two hours ahead of British time: if it is 12.00 in England, it's 14.00 in Greece.

TIPPING

If you have enjoyed your meal and are satisfied with the service, it is usual to leave a 10 per cent tip. It is not necessary to tip taxi drivers, but it is normal to leave them the small change.

WEIGHTS & MEASURES

Greeks use the metric system, showing distances in kilometres (1 km is just over half a mile) and weights in kilograms (1 kg is 2.2 lbs). House wine is normally priced by the kilogram rather than by the litre, which looks odd, but they are the same.

Imperial to metric

1 inch = 2.54 centimetres
1 foot = 30 centimetres
1 mile = 1.6 kilometres
1 ounce = 28 grams
1 pound = 454 grams
1 pint = 0.6 litres
1 gallon = 4.6 litres

Metric to imperial

1 centimetre = 0.4 inches
1 metre = 3 feet, 3 inches
1 kilometre = $\frac{1}{2}$ mile
1 gram = 0.04 ounces
1 kilogram = 2.2 pounds
1 litre = 1.8 pints

INDEX

ACKNOWLEDGEMENTS

We would like to thank all the photographers, picture libraries and organizations for the loan of the photographs reproduced in this book, to whom copyright in the photograph belongs:
B and E Anderson (pages 5, 22, 49, 66, 74, 83, 88, 91);
Ivy Press (page 97);
Jupiter Images Corporation (pages 109, 111, 125);
Pictures Colour Library Ltd (pages 1, 9, 50, 55, 86);
Spectrum Colour Library (page 73);
Thomas Cook Tour Operations Ltd (pages 13, 24, 29, 34, 44, 63, 71, 93, 95, 96, 101, 103, 104, 107, 110).

We would also like to thank the following for their contribution to this series:
John Woodcock (map and symbols artwork);
Becky Alexander, Patricia Baker, Sophie Bevan, Judith Chamberlain-Webber, Stephanie Evans, Nicky Gyopari, Krystyna Mayer, Robin Pridy (editorial support);
Christine Engert, Suzie Johanson, Richard Lloyd, Richard Peters, Alistair Plumb, Jane Prior, Barbara Theisen, Ginny Zeal, Barbara Zuñiga (design support).

Send your thoughts to
books@thomascook.com

- Found a beach bar, peaceful stretch of sand or must-see sight that we don't feature?
- Like to tip us off about any information that needs a little updating?
- Want to tell us what you love about this handy, little guidebook and more importantly how we can make it even handier?

Then here's your chance to tell all! Send us ideas, discoveries and recommendations today and then look out for your valuable input in the next edition of this title. And, as an extra 'thank you' from Thomas Cook Publishing, you'll be automatically entered into our exciting monthly prize draw.

Send an email to the above address or write to:
HotSpots Project Editor, Thomas Cook Publishing, PO Box 227, Unit 15/16, Coningsby Road, Peterborough PE3 8SB, UK.